SCOTT FORESMAN · ADDISON WESLEY

Mathematics

Grade 3

Homework Workbook

PEARSON

Scott
Foresman

Editorial Offices: Glenview, Illinois • Parsippany, New Jersey • New York, New York

Sales Offices: Parsippany, New Jersey • Duluth, Georgia • Glenview, Illinois
Coppell, Texas • Ontario, California • Mesa, Arizona

ISBN 0-328-07558-2

9 10 V011 09 08 07 06

Ways to Use Numbers

Numbers can be used to locate, to name, to measure, and to count.

Locate

Name

Measure

Count

Numbers can also be used to show the order of people or objects. These are called **ordinal numbers**.

Tell if each number is used to locate, name, measure, or count.

1.

_____

2.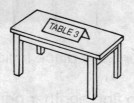

_____

3.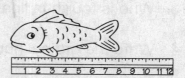

_____

Use the picture below for 4–7.

Striped Dotted Gray Starred White

4. Which ball is third in line?

_____

5. Write an ordinal number for the white ball's place in line.

_____

6. Which ball is second in line?

_____

7. Which ball is fourth in line?

_____

8. **Number Sense** What ordinal number would come next in the following list? 10th, 11th, 12th, . . .

_____

Name_____

Ways to Use Numbers

Tell if each number is used to locate, name, measure, or count.

1.

_____

2.

_____

Sal   Yon   Frank   Joe   Kym   Lia

3. Who is fourth in line?   _____

4. Write the ordinal number for Sal's place in line.   _____

5. **Reasoning** If Joe leaves to find another book,
   who will be fifth in line?   _____

Test Prep

6. Which ordinal number comes next? 42nd, 43rd, 44th, _____

   A. 54th   **B.** 41st   **C.** 45th   **D.** 55th

7. **Writing in Math** Explain how a number can name
   something.

   _____

   _____

   _____

   _____

Name_____

Numbers in the Hundreds

Here are different ways to show 612.

place-value blocks:

expanded form: 600 + 10 + 2

standard form: 612

word form: six hundred twelve

Write each number in standard form.

1. _____

2. _____

3. 400 + 30 + 7   **4.** six hundred twenty   **5.** 200 + 50 + 1

_____   _____   _____

6. three hundred forty-five _____

Write the word form for each number.

7. 285 _____

8. 892 _____

9. 146 _____

10. 378 _____

11. Number Sense Write a three-digit number with a
2 in the hundreds place and a 4 in the tens place. _____

Name_____

Numbers in the Hundreds

Write each number in standard form.

1.

2.

3.

_____   _____   _____

4. $700 + 30 + 6$ _____

5. two hundreds, five tens, nine ones   _____

Write the word name for each number.

6. 212   _____

7. $600 + 3$ _____

Algebra Find each missing number.

8. $200 + 10 + \underline{\quad\quad} = 212$ 9. $\underline{\quad\quad} + 70 + 1 = 971$

Test Prep

10. Which is the missing number? $100 + \underline{\quad\quad} + 9 = 139$

    A. 3   **B.** 13   **C.** 30   **D.** 33

11. **Writing in Math** Explain how the digit 7 can have different values.

_____

_____

_____

_____

Place-Value Patterns

Here are three different ways to show 114.

114 = 1 hundred, 1 ten, 4 ones   114 = 11 tens, 4 ones

114 = 1 hundred, 14 ones

Use place-value blocks to show 140 in two ways. Draw the blocks you use for each answer.

1. Using only hundreds and tens blocks

2. Using only tens blocks

Write each number in standard form.

3.

_____

4.

_____

5. Writing in Math Can you draw 321 using only place-value blocks for hundreds and tens? Explain.

_____

_____

Name_____

Place-Value Patterns

Write each number in standard form.

1.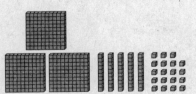

_____

2.

_____

3. **Number Sense** The largest giant jellyfish ever found was
7 ft wide and had tentacles that were more than 120 ft
long. Draw place-value blocks to show 120 using only tens.

4. **Representations** Draw the place-value blocks needed to
finish making 469.

Test Prep

5. Which number has the same value as 4 hundreds, 7 tens,
and 22 ones?

   A. 492   **B.** 472   **C.** 452   **D.** 427

6. **Writing in Math** Explain how you can use place-value
blocks to show 100 in different ways.

_____

_____

_____

Name_____

Numbers in the Thousands

Here are different ways to show 2,263.

place-value blocks:

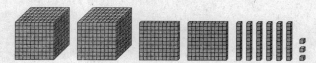

expanded form: 2,000 + 200 + 60 + 3

standard form: 2,263

word form: two thousand, two hundred sixty-three

Write each number in standard form.

1. _____

2. _____

3. 7,000 + 400 + 40 + 8 _____

4. five thousand, seven hundred fifty-five _____

Write each number in expanded form.

5. 1,240 _____

6. 6,381 _____

7. **Number Sense** Write a four-digit number with a
7 in the thousands place and a 6 in the ones place. _____

8. **Reasoning** Jason will build a number with the digits 4, 7, 2,
and 6. In what order should he put the digits if he
wants to make the greatest number possible? _____

Numbers in the Thousands

Write each number in standard form.

1.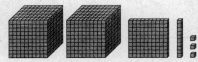

2. $9,000 + 600 + 50 + 4$

_____   _____

3. eight thousand, seven hundred fourteen   _____

Write each number in expanded form.

4. 1,069 _____

5. 2,002 _____

6. **Reasoning** Write a number that can be shown using
only thousands blocks or only hundreds blocks.   _____

Test Prep

7. Fredrick wants to build 1,412 with place-value blocks. He
does not have any thousands blocks. How many hundreds
blocks will he use?

A. 41   **B.** 14   **C.** 4   **D.** 1

8. **Writing in Math** Explain how you know that 6,775 is the
correct answer to the clues below.

- My ones digit is 5.
- My thousands digit is one more than my ones digit.
- My hundreds digit is 7.
- My tens digit is the same as my hundreds digit.

What number am I?

_____

_____

_____

Name_____

Greater Numbers

A period is a group of three digits in a number, starting from the right. A comma is used to separate two periods.

Thousands Period			Ones Period		
hundred thousands	ten thousands	thousands	hundreds	tens	ones
2	4	7 ,	3	6	2

Here are different ways to show 247,362.

expanded form: 200,000 + 40,000 + 7,000 + 300 + 60 + 2

standard form: 247,362

word form: two hundred forty-seven thousand, three hundred sixty-two

Write each number in standard form.

1. 60,000 + 8,000 + 200 + 50 + 1 _____

2. 30,000 + 600 + 30 + 2 _____

3. four hundred one thousand, four hundred fifty-four _____

4. five hundred twenty-nine thousand, three hundred seventy-eight _____

5. Write 522,438 in expanded form.

_____

6. Write 349,281 in expanded form.

_____

7. Number Sense What is the value of the 7 in 86,752? _____

8. Lake Erie is 32,630 square miles. Write the area of Lake Erie in expanded form.

_____

Greater Numbers

Write each number in standard form.

1. seventy-five thousand, three hundred twelve _____

2. one hundred fourteen thousand, seven _____

3. 20,000 + 7,000 + 600 + 90 + 3 _____

4. 100,000 + 40,000 + 2,000 + 500 + 30 + 2 _____

Write each number in expanded form.

5. 73,581 _____

6. 100,317 _____

7. **Number Sense** Write a six-digit number in which the digit 4 has the value of 40,000. _____

8. The area of Ethiopia is 437,600 square miles. Write the area of Ethiopia in expanded form.

   _____

9. The area of Israel is 8,550 square miles. Write the area of Israel in word form.

   _____

Test Prep

10. Which is the value of 3 in 328,469?

    A. 300   **B.** 3,000   **C.** 30,000   **D.** 300,000

11. **Writing in Math** Explain how 8 ten thousands can be equal to 80 thousands.

    _____

    _____

    _____

© Pearson Education, Inc. 3

Name_____

Read and Understand Problems

School Bus Routes Tim's bus travels 5 miles from his house to school. Ann's bus travels 8 miles from her house to school. How many miles do the two buses travel together?

Read and Understand

Step 1: What do you know?

- Tell the problem in your own words. — Each school bus travels a number of miles.

- Identify key facts and details. — Tim's bus travels 5 mi. Ann's bus travels 8 mi.

Step 2: What are you trying to find?

- Tell what the question is asking. — We want to know total miles both buses travel.

- Show the main idea.

5 mi	8 mi
total miles	

Use addition to find the answer. 5 + 8 = 13 mi

Sharing Marbles Jamal had a bag of marbles. He gave 6 red marbles and 3 green marbles to Josh. How many marbles did Jamal give to Josh?

1. Identify key facts and details. _____

_____

2. Tell what the question is asking. _____

_____

4. Show the main idea. Use it to solve the problem.

5. Write your answer in a complete sentence.

_____

_____

© Pearson Education, Inc. 3

6 Use with Lesson 1-6.

Name_____

Read and Understand

Grandchildren Grandma Fee has four children. Each of her children has three children. Seven of Grandma Fee's grandchildren are boys. How many grandchildren does Grandma Fee have?

1. Tell the problem in your own words.

_____

_____

2. Identify key facts and details.

_____

_____

3. Tell what the question is asking.

_____

_____

4. Show the main idea.

5. Solve the problem. Write the answer in a complete sentence.

_____

6. **Bakery** Al's Pet Bakery baked 120 dog biscuits on Monday and 150 dog biscuits on Tuesday. It sold all but 30 of the biscuits and gave half the unsold biscuits to an animal shelter. How many biscuits did it sell? Write the answer in a complete sentence.

_____

Name_____

Comparing Numbers

When you compare numbers, you use these symbols.

< is less than   > is greater than   = is equal to

You can compare numbers using place-value blocks, a number line, or by comparing digits that are in the same place.
Compare 375 and 353.

 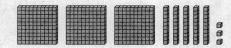

Both have the same number of hundreds.

375 has more tens, so 375 > 353, or 353 < 375.

375 is to the right of 353, so 375 > 353. 353 is to the left of 375, so 353 < 375, or 353 is less than 375. Both have the same number of hundreds. Seven tens is greater than five tens. So, 375 > 353, or 353 < 375.

Compare the numbers. Use <, >, or =. Use any method.

1. 5 ◯ 3   **2.** 39 ◯ 93   **3.** 1,025 ◯ 1,025

4. 842 ◯ 824   **5.** 3,121 ◯ 1,099   **6.** 12,492 ◯ 10,863

7. Writing in Math Every digit in 8,999 is greater than any digit in 24,005. Explain why 24,005 is greater than 8,999.

_____

_____

_____

Name_____

Comparing Numbers

Compare the numbers. Use <, >, or =.

1.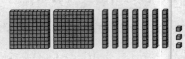

237 ◯ 273

2. 130 ◯ 113

3. 49 ◯ 94

4. 4,218 ◯ 5,723

5. 58,300 ◯ 50,838

6. Between which pair of cities is the distance greater?

_____

_____

Distance in Miles

New York, NY to Rapid City, SD	1,701
Rapid City, SD to Miami, FL	2,167
Miami, FL to Seattle, WA	3,334
Seattle, WA to Portland, OR	173
Portland, OR to Little Rock, AR	2,217

7. Use <, >, or = to compare the distance from Rapid City to Miami to the distance from Portland to Little Rock. _____

8. **Number Sense** Explain why 1,734 is greater than 175.

_____

_____

Test Prep

9. Which number is greater than 238,432?

   A. 238,433   **B.** 23,899   **C.** 238   **D.** 238,431

10. **Writing in Math** Explain how to compare 8,563 and 8,699.

_____

_____

_____

Ordering Numbers

To order numbers from greatest to least or least to greatest, you can use a number line.

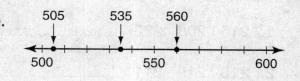

These numbers, in order from least to greatest, are 505, 535, and 560.

You can also use place value to order numbers. First, you compare pairs of numbers to find the greatest number. Then you compare the other numbers.

630 > 305
Is 630 also greater than 555?

630 > _____

National Monument	Total Height
Statue of Liberty	305 ft
Washington Monument	555 ft
Gateway Arch	630 ft

Yes, so 630 is greatest.

555 > _____
So, 305 is least.

Write the numbers in order from least to greatest.

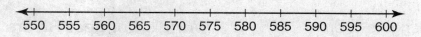

1. 560 583 552   _____

2. 583 575 590   _____

3. 576 580 557   _____

Write the numbers in order from greatest to least.

4. 973 1,007 996   _____

5. 5,626 5,636 5,616   _____

6. 445 455 450   _____

7. **Representations** Jamie is 9 years old, Al is 12 years old, David is 3 years old, and Naomi is 6 years old. Draw a number line from 1 to 12. Put these ages on the number line from least to greatest.

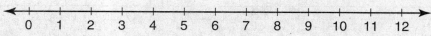

Ordering Numbers

Write the numbers in order from least to greatest.

1. 216 208 222 _____

2. 210 219 211 _____

Write the numbers in order from greatest to least.

3. 633 336 363 _____

4. 5,000 50 500 _____

5. Representations Draw a number line. Make sure the
following numbers are on your number line:
1,472; 1,560; 1,481.

6. Write the river lengths in order
from least to greatest.

_____

_____

_____

World's Longest Rivers

River	Length (miles)
Amazon	4,000
Yangtze	3,964
Mississippi-Missouri	3,740
Nile	4,145

Test Prep

7. In which number does 4 have the greatest value?

A. 9,499 **B.** 4,391 **C.** 2,240 **D.** 1,944

8. Writing in Math Sara says the number with the most digits
is always greatest. Do you agree? Explain.

_____

_____

Number Patterns

You can use a number line to find a number pattern.

Find the pattern. Find the next two numbers.

17, 14, 11, 8, _____ , _____

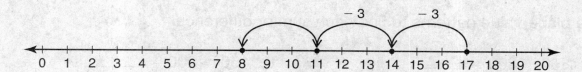

A hundred chart can help you find
39 − 12 using place-value patterns.
Start at 39 and move up one row
to subtract 10. Then move two columns
to the left to subtract 2 ones.
39 − 12 = 27.

1	2	3	4	5	6	7	8	9	10
11	12	13	14	15	16	17	18	19	20
21	22	23	24	25	26	27←28–29			30
31	32	33	34	35	36	37	38	39	40
41	42	43	44	45	46	47	48	49	50
51	52	53	54	55	56	57	58	59	60

Continue each pattern.

1. 4, 8, 12, ☐ , ☐

2. 90, 80, 70, ☐ , ☐

3. 7, 14, 21, ☐ , ☐

4. 25, 50, 75, ☐ , ☐

Use place-value patterns to find each sum or difference.

5. 18 + 20

6. 21 + 17

7. 46 − 12

_____

_____

_____

8. Writing in Math Explain how you can use a hundred chart
to subtract 12 from 46.

_____

_____

_____

_____

Number Patterns

Continue each pattern.

1. 15, 30, 45, _____, _____

2. 30, 24, 18, _____, _____

3. 3, 6, 9, _____, 15

4. 220, 230, 240, _____, _____

Use place-value patterns to find each sum or difference.

5. 890 − 300 = _____

6. 150 + 200 = _____

7. 470 − 350 = _____

8. 340 + 220 = _____

9. Joshua is raising fruit flies for a science project. At the beginning of the first day, he had 4 fruit flies. His fruit flies double in number each day. How many fruit flies does he have at the end of three days?   _____

10. **Representations** Choose your own pattern. Draw a number line to show your pattern.

Test Prep

11. Which is 100 more than 7,399?

A. 7,400   **B.** 7,499   **C.** 8,399   **D.** 8,499

12. **Writing in Math** Mrs. Bradner has 30 tomato plants. She wants to plant the same number of plants in each row of her garden. Explain how she could decide the number of rows to plant.

_____

_____

_____

_____

Rounding Numbers

You can use place value to round to the nearest ten or hundred.

Find the rounding place. If the digit in the ones or the tens place is 5, 6, 7, 8, or 9, then round to the next greater number. If the digit is less than 5, do not change the digit in the rounding place.

Round 17 to the nearest ten: __20__

Explain. __7 is in the ones place. Round to the next greater ten.__

Round 153 to the nearest ten. __150__

Explain. __Because 3 is in the ones place and 3 is less than 5, the digit in the tens place doesn't change.__

Round 1,575 to the nearest hundred. __1,600__

Explain. __Because the 7 in the tens place is 5 or greater, round to the next greater hundred.__

---

1. Round 63 to the nearest ten: _____

Explain. _____

Round each number to the nearest ten.

2. 58

3. 71

4. 927

5. 3,121

_____ _____ _____ _____

Round each number to the nearest hundred.

6. 577

7. 820

8. 2,345

9. 8,750

_____ _____ _____ _____

10. Reasoning If you live 71 mi from a river, does it make sense to say you live about 80 mi from the river? Explain.

_____

Name_____

Rounding Numbers

Round to the nearest ten.

1. 37   **2.** 92   **3.** 133   **4.** 2,219

_____   _____   _____   _____

Round to the nearest hundred.

5. 172   **6.** 929   **7.** 8,438   **8.** 5,555

_____   _____   _____   _____

9. Number Sense Tyrell says $750 is about $800. Sara says $750 is about $700. Who is correct? Explain.

_____

_____

10. Which two lakes have the same depth when rounded to the nearest hundred?

_____

11. Which lake has a depth of about 900 ft?

_____

Depths of the Great Lakes	
Lake	**Depth (feet)**
Erie	210
Huron	750
Michigan	923
Ontario	802
Superior	1,333

Test Prep

12. Round 7,468 to the nearest hundred.

A. 7,400   **B.** 7,460   **C.** 7,470   **D.** 7,500

13. Writing in Math Explain how you would use a number line to round 148 to the nearest ten.

_____

_____

Name_____

Plan and Solve

Hurdle Jumping Rashid and Juan set up a 50 m hurdle race. They set one hurdle at 5 m, one at 45 m, and one at every 5 m in between. How many hurdles will the runners cross?

Step 1: Choose a strategy.

- **Show what you know:** Draw a picture, make an organized list, make a table or graph, use objects/act it out.

- **Look for a Pattern**

- **Try, Check, and Revise**

- **Use Logical Reasoning**

- **Solve a Simpler Problem**

- **Work Backward**

- **Write a Number Sentence**

Step 2: Stuck? Don't give up. Try these.

- Reread the problem.

- Tell the problem in your own words.

- Tell what you know.

- Identify key facts and details.

- Show the main idea.

- Try a different strategy.

- Retrace your steps.

Step 3: Answer the question in the problem.

What strategy can be used? Drawing a picture will help solve this problem.

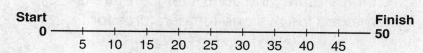

The answer to the problem: The runners will cross 9 hurdles.

Beaded Bracelets Sue is able to make six beaded bracelets each month. If Sue begins on January 1st, how many bracelets will she be able to finish in time for the crafts sale on May 2nd?

1. What strategy might work to solve this problem?

_____

_____

2. Give the answer to the problem in a complete sentence.

_____

_____

PROBLEM-SOLVING SKILL
Plan and Solve

Pyramid Hector has made a pyramid of blocks. He used eight blocks to build the bottom row of the pyramid. All the rows are stacked on top of each other. Each row has one less block than the row it sits on. How many blocks did Hector need to build his pyramid?

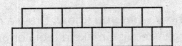

1. Finish the picture to help solve the problem.

2. What strategy was used to solve the problem?

_____

3. Write the answer to the problem in a complete sentence.

_____

Temperature The average temperature in Seattle, Washington, during January is 45°F. February's average temperature is 49°F, with 52°F in March and 58°F in April. May's average temperature is 12°F higher than March's temperature, and June's temperature is 11°F higher than April's. What are the average temperatures for May and June in Seattle?

4. What strategy did you use to solve the problem?

_____

_____

5. Give the answer in a complete sentence.

_____

_____

6. What other strategy could you use to solve the Temperature problem?

_____

Counting Money

You can count on to find the value of coins and bills. When you count money, start with the bills, then follow with the coins of greatest value. This is what you say when you count on to get to $7.52.

Count on: $5.00 $6.00 $7.00

$7.25 $7.50 $7.51 $7.52

Because different coins and bills have different values, an amount of money can be made in different ways. Here are three ways to make $1.01.

+

Write the total value in dollars and cents.

1.

_____

2. What bills and coins could you use to show $8.60?

_____

_____

12 Use with Lesson 1-12.

Name_____

Counting Money

Write the total value in dollars and cents.

1.

_____

2.

_____

3. Tell what bills and coins you could use to make $5.37 in two ways.

_____

_____

_____

4. Tell what coins you would use to show $0.37 using the least amount of coins.

_____

Test Prep

5. Which does not mean 25 cents?

   A. Quarter **B.** $25 **C.** 25¢ **D.** $0.25

6. **Writing in Math** Explain how $0.60 can be shown two different ways using only three coins each time.

_____

_____

Name_____

Making Change

Suppose you bought a sandwich that costs $3.75 and gave the clerk a $5 bill. The clerk might first say "$3.75." Then he or she might hand you a quarter and say "$4.00," then hand you a dollar and say "$5.00." The clerk counted on from the price of your item to the amount you paid with to find your change.

$3.75 $4.00 $5.00

Your change would be $1.25.

Use the School Cafeteria menu to the right. List the coins and bills you would use to make change. Then write the change in dollars and cents.

School Cafeteria Menu	
Daily Special	$3.49
Fruit Cup	$1.95
Salad	$2.09
Corn Muffin	$1.50
Milk	$0.75

1. Emilio bought a corn muffin with two $1 bills.

_____

_____

2. Marco bought a Daily Special with a $5 bill.

_____

_____

3. Number Sense Craig bought a milk with a $1 bill. Write two different ways he could receive his change.

_____

_____

4. Reasoning Andrea bought a salad and a milk. She got a dime, a nickel, a penny, and two $1 bills in change. How much did Andrea give the clerk? _____

Making Change

List the bills and coins you would use to make change.
Then write the change in dollars and cents.

1. Seth paid for a $0.29 eraser with $0.50.

_____

2. A new hair clip costs $1.60. Janice paid for a hair clip with
two dollar bills.

_____

3. **Reasoning** If pencils cost $0.26 each, could you buy four
pencils with $1.00? Explain.

_____

_____

4. **Algebra** Alice bought an ice cream cone for
$0.78. She got $0.02 change. How much money
did Alice give the cashier?   _____

Test Prep

5. Martha used a dollar bill to pay for her $0.48 baseball card.
Which does not show the proper change?

A.   **B.**

C.   **D.**

6. **Writing in Math** Braden and Bialy each bought a kazoo
for $0.89. They each paid with a $1.00 bill. Explain two
different ways to show their change.

_____

_____

Name_____

Look Back and Check

Planting Flowers Max had 120 bulbs to plant in the fall. There were 48 daffodil bulbs, and the rest were tulip bulbs. How many tulip bulbs did Max have to plant?

You are not finished with the problem until you look back and check your answer.

Paige's Work

120	
48	?

120 – 48 = 72
Max planted 72 tulip bulbs.

Step 1: Check your answer.
Did Paige answer the right question?
Yes, she found the number of tulip bulbs Max planted.

Step 2: Check your work.
Paige could use place-value patterns to check if her answer is correct.
She can use a number line to skip count by 10s.

Did Paige use the correct operation?
Paige used subtraction to find the number of tulip bulbs Max planted.

Camera Sales A camera company wants to sell at least 130 cameras each week. One week they sold 38 cameras with zoom lenses and 86 regular cameras. Did they sell at least 130 cameras that week?

Martin's Work

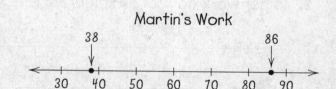

I know that 38 can be rounded to 40 and 86 can be rounded to 90.

40 + 90 = 130: Yes. The camera store sold enough cameras.

1. Did Martin answer the right question? Explain.

_____

_____

_____

2. Is his work correct? Explain.

_____

_____

_____

Name_____

PROBLEM-SOLVING SKILL
Look Back and Check

Pumpkin Seeds Ricardo planted 22 pumpkin seeds in hills. He planted 2 seeds in each hill. How many hills did he plant seeds in?

Esther solved the Pumpkin Seed problem. Check her work.

2	2	2	2	2	2	2	2	2	2	2

11 hills

1. Did Esther answer the right question? Explain.

_____

_____

2. Is her work correct? Explain.

_____

_____

Gardening Tedo makes $0.75 an hour weeding gardens. How much will he make if he works for four hours?

Joshua solved the Gardening problem. Check his work.

3. Did Joshua answer the right question? Explain.

_____

_____

_____

Tedo's Pay

Hours	Pay
1	$0.75
2	$1.50
3	$2.00
4	$2.75

He will make $2.75 in four hours.

4. Is his answer correct? Explain.

_____

_____

Name_____

White-Tailed Deer

White-tailed deer that live in the desert weigh less than their eastern relatives. The average weight of an adult male Desert White-tailed deer is about 200 pounds. The females have an average weight of about 125 pounds. Use place value to compare.

200

2 hundreds is greater than
1 hundred.

125

You could say 200 > 125, or 125 < 200.

So, the male white-tailed deer weighs more than the female white-tailed deer.

White-tailed deer can run as fast as 40 miles per hour. Suppose the speed of one deer is recorded at 37 miles per hour. The speed of another deer is recorded at 23 miles per hour.

1. Compare the speeds of the two deer, using the > and < symbols.

   _____

2. How much faster did the first deer run than the second deer? Show your work and write your answer in a complete sentence.

   _____

   _____

   _____

3. Nena paid $4.75 to hike in a state park for one day. She paid with a $20 bill. How much change did she receive?

   _____

Name_____

Great Heights

There are many very tall mountains in the United States. The table shows the heights of a few of the tallest mountains.

Mountains in the United States

Mountain	Height (feet)
Mount McKinley	20,320
Mount Massive	14,421
Mount Rainier	14,410

1. Write the word form of the height of Mount Rainier.

_____

_____

2. Write the expanded form of the height of Mount Massive.

_____

3. Order the heights from greatest to least.

_____

4. Leonard would like to buy a fruit juice that costs $0.95.
   Leonard has five coins that equal that amount exactly.
   Tell what coins Leonard has.

_____

_____

Reba would also like to buy a fruit juice. She decides to buy one for herself and one for her friend Yvonne.

5. The two juices cost $1.90. If Reba pays for them with $10.00, how much change should she receive? _____

6. Tell two different ways Reba could receive her change.

_____

_____

Name_____

Addition Properties

The Commutative (order) Property

You can add numbers in any order, and the sum will be the same.

6 + 2 = 8

2 + 6 = 8

The Associative (grouping) Property

You can group addends in any way, and the sum will be the same.

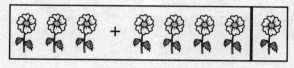

(3 + 4) + 1 = 8

3 + (4 + 1) = 8

The Identity (zero) Property

The sum of any number and zero equals that same number.

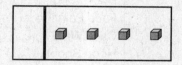

0 + 4 = 4

Find each sum.

1. 3 + (2 + 4) = _____

2. (0 + 5) + 2 = _____

3. (8 + 3) + 4 = _____

4. 9 + 2 + 6 = _____

Write each missing number.

5. 3 + 4 = 4 + _____

6. _____ + 7 = 7

7. (2 + 3) + 4 = _____ + (2 + 4)

8. 9 + (2 + 7) = (9 + 2) + _____

9. Reasoning Does (4 + 5) + 2 = 9 + 2? Explain.

_____

_____

Name_____

Addition Properties

Find each sum.

1. $(4 + 2) + 1 =$ _____

2. $6 + (2 + 1) =$ _____

3. $6 + 1 + 5 =$ _____

4. $4 + 3 + 7 =$ _____

Write each missing number.

5. $7 + 2 = 2 +$ _____

6. $3 + 0 = 0 +$ _____

7. $(2 + 4) + 5 = 2 + ($ _____ $+ 5)$

8. $3 + (7 + 1) = 3 +$ _____

9. **Number Sense** Write a number sentence with 3 addends whose sum is 14.

_____

10. Alex played the Duck Pond, the Cake Walk, and the Hoop Shoot. How many tickets did he use?

_____

Games	
Duck Pond	2 tickets
Face Painting	4 tickets
Cake Walk	3 tickets
Hoop Shoot	1 ticket
Wheel Spin	2 tickets

11. Patsy did the Cake Walk twice before she won a cake. Then she played the Wheel Spin one time and won a pencil. How many tickets did she use?

_____

Test Prep

12. Which property is shown by $5 + 2 = 2 + 5$?

    A. Identity Property

    B. Associative Property

    C. Commutative Property

    D. Distributive Property

13. **Writing in Math** Jake says adding 0 does not change a number. Is he correct? Explain.

_____

_____

_____

Relating Addition and Subtraction

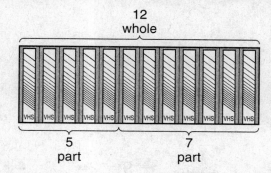

When you know the parts and the whole, you can write a fact family. Here is a fact family that uses the numbers 5, 7, and 12.

$5 + 7 = 12$ $12 - 5 = 7$

$7 + 5 = 12$ $12 - 7 = 5$

Complete each fact family.

1. $3 + 5 =$ _____ $8 -$ _____ $= 3$

_____ $+ 3 = 8$ _____ $- 3 = 5$

2. $9 + 2 =$ _____ $11 -$ _____ $= 9$

_____ $+ 9 = 11$ _____ $- 9 = 2$

Find each missing number.

3. $7 +$ _____ $= 14$ **4.** _____ $+ 5 = 11$

5. $4 +$ _____ $= 12$ **6.** $6 +$ _____ $= 15$

7. Number Sense Write a subtraction fact using 6 such as $6 - \blacksquare = \blacksquare$. Then write an addition fact you could use to check it.

_____

_____

_____

Name_____

Relating Addition and Subtraction

Complete each fact family.

1. 3 + 6 = _____

    6 + _____ = 9

    9 − _____ = 3

    _____ − 3 = 6

2. 2 + 9 = _____

    _____ + 2 = 11

    11 − 2 = _____

    _____ − 9 = 2

Find each missing number.

3. 7 + _____ = 13   **4.** 9 + _____ = 19   **5.** 8 + _____ = 12

6. Number Sense Write the fact family for 3, 9, and 12.

_____

_____

_____

7. Write the fact family for the total number of dots on the domino.

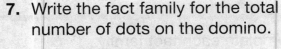

_____

_____

_____

_____

Test Prep

8. Which number sentence does not belong in the fact family?

  A. 4 + 9 = 13   **B.** 13 − 4 = 9   **C.** 9 − 4 = 5   **D.** 9 + 4 = 13

9. Writing in Math Write a fact family with a sum of 17. Explain how you picked the addends.

_____

_____

_____

Find a Rule

In	1	3	2	4	8	6
Out	0	2	1	3	7	

Each number in the top row, **In,** of the table is related to the number in the bottom row, **Out,** by the same rule. The rule in this table is **subtract 1.** A rule explains what to do to the numbers that you put **In,** like those on the top row of the table, to get the numbers that come **Out.**

Complete the table.

1.

In	4	3	1	5	2	7
Out	7	6	4	8		

2. Write the rule, such as **subtract 1.** _____

Complete each table. Then write a rule for the table.

3.

In	5	20	15	10	30
Out	10	25	20		

Rule: _____

4.

In	16	17	10	13	11
Out	9	10	3		

Rule: _____

5. Writing in Math The rule is **add 4.** Make your own table with an In and Out pattern to match the rule.

Find a Rule

Complete each table. Then write a rule for the table.

1.

In	7	13	4	12	0
Out	11	17	8		

2.

In	16	9	4	18	3
Out	13	6	1		

3.

In	16	31	27	62	99
Out	26	41	37		

4.

In	57	39	71	22	19
Out	46	28	60		

5. **Number Sense** Lako put in 12 and got out 17. Then she put in 1 and got out 6. What rule was she using?

6. Elton uses the rule Subtract 6 for his table. If he puts in 18, what will he get out?

Test Prep

7. The rule for Stan's table is Subtract 4. Which number should he put in to get out 7?

   A. 13   **B.** 11   **C.** 9   **D.** 3

8. **Writing in Math** Angel says the rule for this table is Add 0. Frank says the rule is Subtract 0. Who is correct? Explain.

In	6	14	31	29	0
Out	6	14	31	29	0

Write a Number Sentence

Suppose you do two tasks today. How much money would you earn if you walked the dog and made your bed?

To write a number sentence to solve a problem, follow these four steps:

Task	Pay
Walk Dog	$2.00
Do Dishes	$1.25
Make Bed	$1.00

Step 1: Show the main idea.

n	
$2.00	$1.00

You must add to find the missing sum.

Step 2: Decide which operation fits the main idea.

Step 3: Use a letter to show what you are trying to find.

The *n* shows how much money you will make.

Step 4: Solve the number sentence.

$2 + $1 = n
You will make $3.

Finally, look back and check your answer. Is your answer reasonable? $2 + $1 = $3. Yes, it is reasonable.

Use the task price list. Write a number sentence with a variable. Then solve.

1. Tommy did the dishes and made his bed. How much money did Tommy earn?

_____

2. Alice gets $5 allowance each week. Her parents take away money from her allowance if she does not do tasks. This week Alice forgot to make her bed twice. How much allowance will Alice get this week?

_____

3. **Writing in Math** Write a word problem using the task price list. Then solve your problem. Explain how you know your answer is correct.

_____

Name_____

PROBLEM-SOLVING STRATEGY

Write a Number Sentence

Write a number sentence. Then solve. Write the answer in a complete sentence.

1. Hector bought 9 lb of dog food. His dog ate 3 lb in one week. How much dog food was left?

_____

_____

2. Janice pulled weeds for 2 hr on Saturday and 1 hr on Sunday. She watered the garden for 1 hr. How much time did she spend pulling weeds?

_____

_____

Heather has a new bead kit. It has directions for many different crafts. Help her decide how many beads to use. For 3–6, use the craft chart. Write your answer in a complete sentence.

Craft	Red Beads	Blue Beads
Necklace	10	12
Ankle chain	9	11
Key chain	24	16

3. How many beads in all does Heather need to make an ankle chain?

_____

_____

4. Heather will make a key chain and a necklace. How many blue beads will she use?

_____

_____

5. Heather has 17 blue beads. If she makes an ankle chain, how many blue beads will she have left?

_____

_____

6. How many beads in all does Heather need to make a key chain?

_____

_____

Name _____

Mental Math:
Break Apart Numbers

You can break apart numbers to make them easier to add mentally.

Find 31 + 45 using mental math.
There are two ways.

First, break apart the numbers into tens and ones.   **or**   Break apart only one number.

	tens		ones
31 =	30	+	1
45 =	40	+	5

Add the tens together: 30 + 40 = 70.

Add the ones together: 1 + 5 = 6.

Finally, add the tens and the ones together: 70 + 6 = 76.

So, 31 + 45 = 76.

Break apart only one number.

45 = 40 + 5

Then add 40 + 31 = 71.

Next add the 5 to 71:

71 + 5 = 76

So, 31 + 45 = 76.

Find each sum using mental math.

1. 52 + 12 = _____   **2.** 24 + 71 = _____   **3.** 36 + 43 = _____

4. 47 + 50 = _____   **5.** 54 + 23 = _____   **6.** 24 + 72 = _____

7. 33 + 46 = _____   **8.** 22 + 64 = _____   **9.** 34 + 53 = _____

10. Number Sense To add 32 + 56, Juanita first added
32 + 50. What numbers should she add next? _____

11. In June, 46 cars were sold. There were 12 cars sold in April.
How many more cars were sold in June than in April?

_____

Name_____

Mental Math: Break Apart Numbers

Find each sum using mental math.

1. 12 + 36 = _____

2. 42 + 37 = _____

3. 15 + 23 = _____

4. 17 + 42 = _____

5. 84 + 11 = _____

6. 52 + 35 = _____

7. **Number Sense** Ashton broke apart a number
   into 30 + 7. What number did she start with?   _____

For 8 and 9, use the menu and mental math.

8. How much would an Orange Smoothie
   and a Peach Parfait cost?

   _____

Drink Menu	
Strawberry Fizz	$0.45
Orange Smoothie	$0.31
Banana Blast	$0.11
Apple Cider Slush	$0.24
Peach Parfait	$0.46

9. Sarah wants two Apple Cider Slushes.
   How much will she pay?

   _____

Test Prep

10. To break apart the number 42, which two numbers would
    you use?

    A. 40 + 20   **B.** 35 + 3   **C.** 40 + 2   **D.** 20 + 4

11. **Writing in Math** Explain how you would use mental math
    to add 14 + 71.

    _____

    _____

    _____

    _____

Name_____

Mental Math: Using Tens to Add

To add mentally, you can break numbers apart to make a ten.

For example, to find 26 + 17, you can break the numbers apart like this:

A. 26 + 17

B. You can break 17 into 4 + 13.

4 + 13

C. Add 26 + 4 = 30.

26 + 4 = 30

D. Then add 30 + 13 = 43.

30 + 13 = 43

So, 26 + 17 = 43.

To find 46 + 9, you could first find 46 + 10 = 56. Then you can subtract 1 from the answer. 56 − 1 = 55. This is the same sum as 46 + 9.

Find each sum using mental math.

1. 67 + 9 = _____ **2.** 35 + 8 = _____ **3.** 46 + 7 = _____

4. 25 + 49 = _____ **5.** 37 + 56 = _____ **6.** 87 + 13 = _____

7. Reasonableness Marcie says, "To find 87 + 7, I can find 87 + 10 and then subtract 3." Do you agree? Explain?

_____

_____

_____

_____

Mental Math: Using Tens to Add

Find each sum using mental math.

1. $72 + 19 =$ _____

2. $36 + 28 =$ _____

3. $14 + 26 =$ _____

4. $17 + 49 =$ _____

5. $4 + 27 =$ _____

6. $55 + 37 =$ _____

7. Number Sense Jonah wants to add $43 + 19$.
He added $43 + 20$. What step should he take next? _____

In the United States House of Representatives, the number of representatives a state has depends on the number of people living in the state. Use mental math to find each answer.

State	Representatives
California	52
New York	31
Texas	30
Florida	23

8. How many representatives do California and Texas have altogether?

_____

9. How many representatives do Florida and New York have altogether?

_____

10. Reasonableness Miles says $47 + 36$ is the same as $50 + 33$. Is this reasonable? Explain.

_____

_____

Test Prep

11. Find the sum of $27 + 42$ using mental math.

A. 69   **B.** 67   **C.** 62   **D.** 15

12. Writing in Math How does knowing $30 + 7 = 37$ help you find $37 + 23$?

_____

Estimating Sums

Suppose your class is saving 275 cereal box tops for a fundraising project. Your class has 138 Fruity Cereal box tops and 152 Bran Cereal box tops. Does your class have enough box tops for the project? Since you only need to know if you have enough, you can estimate.

Here are some ways you can estimate.

Rounding: Round each addend to the nearest hundred or to the nearest ten. Then add and compare.

Round to the nearest *hundred*.

$$152 \Rightarrow 200$$
$$+138 \Rightarrow 100$$
$$= 300$$

Since 300 > 275, you have enough.

Round to the nearest *ten*.

$$152 \Rightarrow 150$$
$$+138 \Rightarrow 140$$
$$= 290$$

Since 290 > 275, you have enough.

Front-end estimation: Use the front digit of each number and zeroes for the rest.

$$152 \Rightarrow 100$$
$$+138 \Rightarrow 100$$
$$= 200 < 275$$

Compatible numbers: Use numbers that are close but easy to add.

$$152 \Rightarrow 150$$
$$+138 \Rightarrow 140$$
$$= 290 > 275$$

Round to the nearest ten to estimate each sum.

1. 37 + 117 _____

2. 42 + 98 _____

Round to the nearest hundred to estimate each sum.

3. 240 + 109 _____

4. 87 + 588 _____

5. Reasonableness Sun-Yi estimated 270 + 146 and got 300. Is this reasonable? Explain.

_____

_____

_____

Name_____

Estimating Sums

Round to the nearest hundred to estimate each sum.

1. 236 + 492 _____

2. 126 + 223 _____

Round to the nearest ten to estimate each sum.

3. 18 + 36 _____

4. 145 + 239 _____

Use any method to estimate each sum.

5. 167 + 449 _____

6. 387 + 285 _____

7. Number Sense April needs to estimate the sum of 427
and 338. Should she round to the nearest ten or to the
nearest hundred to get the closer answer? Explain.

_____

_____

8. The flower shop just received a shipment of 432 roses.
They need to fill an order for 273 roses. Use any method to
estimate how many roses they will have left.

_____

Test Prep

9. Which of the following shows estimating 287 + 491 by
using compatible numbers?

A. 200 + 500   **B.** 300 + 500   **C.** 280 + 400   **D.** 290 + 490

10. Writing in Math How can you use rounding to estimate 331 + 193?

_____

Overestimates and Underestimates

Overestimate: An overestimate happens when you round up.

Gina has 36 tomato plants and 57 pepper plants. If she has 100 pots, does she have enough for the plants? Round to the nearest ten to estimate the sum.

        36 rounds up to 40
    + 57 rounds up to 60
                        100   She has enough pots.

Each addend was rounded *up* so the estimated sum is *greater than* the actual sum. It is an overestimate.

Underestimates: An underestimate happens when you round down.

Gerry is in charge of seating for the school show. She has set up 34 seats in the center and 23 seats on each side. She is expecting 70 people. Has she set up enough chairs? Round to the nearest ten to estimate the sum.

        34 rounds down to 30
        23 rounds down to 20
    + 23 rounds down to 20
                          70 seats is the estimated sum.

Each addend was rounded *down*, so the estimated sum, 70, is *less than* the actual sum. It is an underestimate.

Estimate each sum by rounding to the nearest ten. Then tell whether each estimate is an overestimate or an underestimate.

1. 36 + 47 _____

2. 11 + 44 _____

3. Number Sense Liz wants to send two packages. The shipping cost for one package will be $42, and the other will cost $38. Liz has $100. Estimate the total cost of shipping the packages. Does Liz have enough money? Explain.

_____

_____

Name_____

Overestimates and Underestimates

Estimate each sum by rounding. Then tell whether each
estimate is an overestimate or an underestimate.

1. 17 + 49   _____

2. 71 + 13   _____

3. 818 + 139   _____

4. 162 + 72   _____

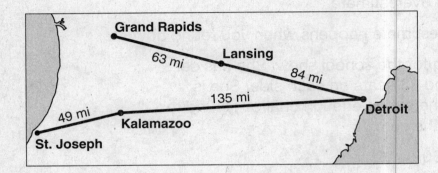

5. Estimate the distance
from Grand Rapids
to Detroit by rounding.

_____

_____

6. Did you underestimate or overestimate?   _____

7. Stanton needs to travel from Detroit to St. Joseph. He says
he will drive more than 190 mi. Do you agree? Explain.

_____

Test Prep

8. Which is an underestimate?

   A. 89 + 139 is about 230.   **B.** 104 + 212 is about 310.

   C. 58 + 77 is about 140.   **D.** 437 + 15 is about 460.

9. Writing in Math Is it reasonable to say the sum of 146 and
149 is less than 300? Explain.

_____

_____

Name_____

Mental Math:
Using Tens to Subtract

You can change numbers to tens to make subtraction problems easier.

There are two ways we can subtract 42 − 28.

One way to make this problem simpler is to change 28 to 30, because it is easier to subtract 30 from 42.

Then, add 2 to the answer because you subtracted 2 too many.
42 − 28 = (42 − 30) + 2 = 14

Another way is to add the same amount to each number.

$$42 - 28$$
$$\Downarrow \quad \Downarrow$$
$$+2 \quad +2$$
$$\Downarrow \quad \Downarrow$$
$$44 - 30 = 14$$

So, 42 − 28 = 14.

Find each difference using mental math.

1. 32 − 17 = _____   **2.** 51 − 46 = _____   **3.** 42 − 17 = _____

4. 29 − 17 = _____   **5.** 63 − 56 = _____   **6.** 78 − 19 = _____

7. 94 − 18 = _____   **8.** 55 − 33 = _____   **9.** 87 − 24 = _____

10. Number Sense To solve 39 − 27, Anika changed it to (40 − 27) + 1. Is this a simpler problem? Explain.

_____

_____

_____

Mental Math:
Using Tens to Subtract

Find each difference using mental math.

1. 63 − 19 = _____

2. 47 − 18 = _____

3. 72 − 38 = _____

4. 61 − 25 = _____

5. 84 − 29 = _____

6. 80 − 11 = _____

7. Number Sense Gillian started solving 88 − 29. This is what she did.

$$88 - 29 = ?$$
$$88 - 30 = 58$$

What should she do next? _____

8. Mary has $84 in her bank account. She withdraws $67. Use mental math to find out how much she has left in her bank account.

9. Tiffany needs 63 tiles for her art mosaic. She has already collected 46 tiles. Use mental math to find how many more tiles she needs.

_____

_____

Test Prep

10. To solve 35 − 19, Jack used 35 − 20 and then

A. added 1.　　**B.** subtracted 1.　　**C.** subtracted 9.　　**D.** added 9.

11. Writing in Math Tell how to find 81 − 36 using mental math.

_____

_____

_____

Mental Math: Counting On to Subtract

Erica wanted to find a new way to subtract mentally. She wondered if counting on would help her to subtract. When you count on, you change a subtraction problem into an addition problem that is missing an addend.

Erica thought that to find 86 − 47, she would change the problem into 47 + ■ = 86.

First, she would count by ones up to the nearest ten: 47 + 3 = 50.

Then, she would count by tens up to 80: 50 + 30 = 80.

Then she counted up to 86: 80 + 6 = 86.

Finally Erica added all the numbers she counted up by: 3 + 30 + 6 = 39.

So, 86 − 47 = 39.

Count on to find each difference mentally.

1. 60 − 32 = _____   2. 48 − 12 = _____   3. 53 − 17 = _____

4. 69 − 24 = _____   5. 76 − 37 = _____   6. 42 − 28 = _____

7. 96 − 85 = _____   8. 56 − 28 = _____   9. 84 − 69 = _____

Algebra Count on to find the value of the missing number.

10. 37 + _____ = 59   11. 76 + _____ = 90   12. 48 + _____ = 65

13. **Number Sense** Rob wants to spend $60 on birthday presents for Samir. Rob buys Samir a hat that costs $37. How much money does Rob have left to buy Samir another birthday present? Write the number sentence you would use to solve the problem. Then solve.

_____

Mental Math: Counting On to Subtract

Count on to find each difference mentally.

1. $43 - 16 =$ _____   **2.** $81 - 67 =$ _____

3. $72 - 16 =$ _____   **4.** $21 - 9 =$ _____

5. $33 - 18 =$ _____   **6.** $65 - 12 =$ _____

Algebra Count on to find the value of the missing number.

7. $37 + x = 59$ _____   **8.** $17 + n = 72$ _____   **9.** $48 + y = 67$ _____

Victoria has saved 73 tokens from the toy store. The tokens can be turned in for prizes. Victoria checked the toy store's Web site to see what prizes were available. The chart at the right shows her choices.

Flying disc	19 tokens
Beach ball	26 tokens
Sunglasses	39 tokens
Beach towel	58 tokens

10. How many tokens will Victoria have left if she gets the beach towel?

11. How many tokens would Victoria have left if she got the beach ball and the sunglasses?

_____   _____

Test Prep

12. Which subtraction problem could be solved by thinking of

$28 +$ _____ $= 45$?

A. $28 - 45$ **B.** $45 - 28$ **C.** $28 - 9$ **D.** $45 - 10$

13. **Writing in Math** Write a missing addend addition sentence to help solve $78 - 49$. Explain how you would use it.

_____

_____

_____

Estimating Differences

Members of the Biology Club caught 136 grasshoppers and
188 butterflies in nets. How many more butterflies than
grasshoppers did the club catch?

Here are four different ways to estimate differences.

Round to the nearest hundred:

188 rounds to 200
− 136 rounds to 100

About 100 more butterflies than
grasshoppers

Round to the nearest ten:

188 rounds to 190
− 136 rounds to 140

About 50 more butterflies than
grasshoppers

Use compatible numbers:

188 is close to 185
− 136 is close to 135

About 50 more butterflies than
grasshoppers

Use front-end estimation:

188 ⇒ 100
− 136 ⇒ 100

About the same number of
butterflies and grasshoppers

Use any method to estimate each difference.

1. 68 − 42 _____

2. 88 − 17 _____

3. 442 − 112 _____

4. 346 − 119 _____

5. 692 − 87 _____

6. 231 − 109 _____

7. Writing in Math Chuck estimated 287 − 29 and got a
difference of about 200. Is this a reasonable estimate? Explain.

_____

_____

_____

_____

Estimating Differences

Round to the nearest hundred to estimate each difference.

1. 236 − 119 _____

2. 558 − 321 _____

Round to the nearest ten to estimate each difference.

3. 677 − 421 _____

4. 296 − 95 _____

Use any method to estimate each difference.

5. 667 − 329

_____

6. 882 − 651

_____

7. Number Sense Fern rounded to the nearest ten to find 548 − 132. She thought 540 − 130 = 410. Do you agree? Explain.

_____

8. Hector's music teacher requires 450 min of practice each month. Hector practiced 239 min the first three weeks this month. Estimate how many minutes he has left to practice.

_____

Test Prep

9. Which is not a compatible number for 76?

A. 80   **B.** 75   **C.** 70   **D.** 60

10. Writing in Math Below are Kate's and Kirk's estimates for 177 − 129. Whose answer is closer to the actual answer? Explain.

Kate: 180 − 130 = 50
Kirk: 200 − 100 = 100

Name_____

You can explain your answer to a problem by breaking the problem into steps. For example:

If you wanted to go on the pony ride and the Ferris wheel, would you need more than 40 tickets?

Carnival Ride Costs

Ferris Wheel	23 tickets
Pony Ride	24 tickets
Water Slide	18 tickets
Moonwalk	12 tickets

Ask yourself if an exact answer or an estimate is needed.

The problem asks if you need more than 40 tickets. An exact answer is not needed. An estimate is enough.

Then, decide which operation you should use and why.

To solve this problem, you should add because you are putting together the number of tickets needed.

Finally, find the answer and explain how you found it.

Step 1: *Round 24 down to 20*

Step 2: *Round 23 down to 20*

Step 3: *20 + 20 = 40*

Step 4: *Both numbers were rounded down, so more than 40 tickets are needed.*

1. Joe wants to go on the water slide and the pony ride. How many tickets will he need? Explain how he can find the exact number of tickets using mental math.

_____

_____

2. Renaldo read a book that has 286 pages. Roz read 179 pages of a different book. About how many more pages did Renaldo read than Roz? Show the problem you used to find the answer.

_____

Name_____

PROBLEM-SOLVING SKILL

Writing to Explain

Snacks The school is going to give each student at Rose Elementary School a granola bar for a snack during field day. There are 758 students. They have already purchased 439 granola bars. About how many more granola bars do they need?

1. Is an exact answer or an estimate needed for this problem? Explain.

_____

2. What operation is needed to solve this problem? Why?

_____

3. What is the answer?

_____

_____

4. Use mental math to find the exact number of granola bars they still need to purchase.

_____

5. Draw a picture to show why you subtracted to solve the problem.

6. **Writing in Math** Explain how the digit 1 can have different values in 111.

_____

_____

_____

_____

PROBLEM-SOLVING APPLICATIONS
Big Cats

The tiger is the largest animal in the cat family and the only cat that consistently has stripes.

There used to be 8 kinds of tigers. Three of the kinds have become extinct, or disappeared.

How many kinds of tigers are left?

You can subtract to find the answer.

$8 - 3 = 5$

So, there are 5 kinds of tigers left.

Suppose a tiger eats 33 lb of meat one night and 39 lb of meat on another night.

1. Round 33 and 39 to the nearest tens place. _____

2. Find the sum of the rounded numbers. _____

3. How many pounds of meat did the tiger eat in the two nights? Show your work and write your answer in a complete sentence.

_____

_____

Suppose Country A has 288 tigers in zoos and Country B has 171 tigers in zoos. How many more tigers does Country A have than Country B?

4. Find an estimate by rounding each number to the nearest ten. _____

5. Find the actual difference. Write your answer in a complete sentence.

_____

_____

Fire Trucks

For 1–3, use the Key Facts: Ladder Trucks chart.

1. Use mental math to find the number of people who can sit in three fire trucks.

_____

2. Write the word name for the length of the hose on a ladder truck.

_____

3. Estimate the difference between the maximum ladder height and the truck length. Explain how you estimated.

_____

_____

_____

KEY FACTS Ladder Trucks	
• Truck width	8 ft
• Truck length	37 ft
• Maximum ladder height	105 ft
• Water spray per minute	1,500 gal
• Seating	6 people
• Hose length	1,000 ft
• Hose width	5 in.

For 4 and 5, use the Firefighting Models chart.

4. Marcy has $10. Does she have enough money to buy an aerial ladder and a fire chief car? Why or why not?

_____

_____

_____

5. Diego bought one of each type of model. How much money did he spend?

_____

Firefighting Models

Model	Price
Pumper	$5
Aerial ladder	$8
Fire chief car	$4
Rescue unit	$6

Adding Two-Digit Numbers

To find 27 + 57, first estimate. 27 is close to 30. 57 is close to 60. 30 + 60 = 90, so the answer should be about 90.

Add the ones. Then add the tens.	Tens	Ones	$\begin{array}{r} 27 \\ +57 \\ \hline 14 \\ 70 \\ \hline 84 \end{array}$
• Add the ones. 7 + 7 = 14 ones			
• Add the tens. 5 tens + 2 tens = 7 tens			
7 tens = _____		70 + 14 = 84	
• Find the sum. 14 + 70 = 84			

Add the ones, then regroup the sum into tens and ones.	Tens	Ones	$\begin{array}{r} 1 \\ 27 \\ +57 \\ \hline 84 \end{array}$
• Add the ones. 7 + 7 = 14 ones			
• Regroup 14 ones into 1 ten, 4 ones.			
• Add the tens. 1 ten + 2 tens + 5 tens = 8 tens 8 tens = 80		14 ones = 1 ten, 4 ones	
• Find the sum.	70	70 + 10 + 4 = 84	

1. $\begin{array}{r} 28 \\ + 34 \\ \hline \end{array}$

2. $\begin{array}{r} 56 \\ + 22 \\ \hline \end{array}$

3. $\begin{array}{r} 84 \\ + 17 \\ \hline \end{array}$

4. $\begin{array}{r} 49 \\ + 72 \\ \hline \end{array}$

5. $\begin{array}{r} 26 \\ + 19 \\ \hline \end{array}$

6. $\begin{array}{r} 65 \\ + 23 \\ \hline \end{array}$

7. $\begin{array}{r} 22 \\ + 79 \\ \hline \end{array}$

8. $\begin{array}{r} 38 \\ + 85 \\ \hline \end{array}$

9. **Reasonableness** Hannah added 65 and 26 and got 81. Is this answer reasonable? Explain.

_____

Name_____

Adding Two-Digit Numbers

1.   73
    + 19

2.   16
    + 48

3.   52
    + 39

4.   28
    + 8

5.   62
    + 19

6.   14
    + 32

7.   59
    + 27

8.   36
    + 26

9. $58 + 28 =$ _____

10. $13 + 72 =$ _____

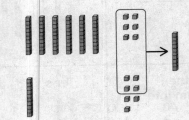

11. **Number Sense** Tad's place-value blocks are shown at the right. What two numbers is he adding?

_____

12. What is the answer to Tad's problem? _____

13. Esther swam 18 laps on Monday and 13 laps on Tuesday. How many laps did she swim in all? _____

14. Write an addition sentence with the sum of 42. One of the addends must have a 4 in the ones column.

_____

_____

Test Prep

15. Which is the sum of $72 + 25$?

   A. 99   **B.** 97   **C.** 90   **D.** 79

16. **Writing in Math** How can estimating help you add two-digit numbers?

_____

_____

Models for Adding Three-Digit Numbers

Find 152 + 329.

Step 1: Show each number with place-value blocks.

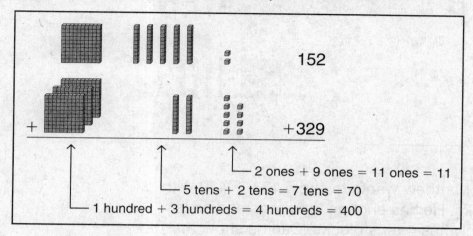

152

+329

2 ones + 9 ones = 11 ones = 11

5 tens + 2 tens = 7 tens = 70

1 hundred + 3 hundreds = 4 hundreds = 400

Step 2: Combine the ones. $2 + 9 = 11$

Step 3: Combine the tens. $50 + 20 = 70$

Step 4: Combine the hundreds. $100 + 300 = 400$

Step 5: Add. $400 + 70 + 11 = 481$

Write each problem and find the sum.

1. _____

2. _____

3. _____

4. _____

Models for Adding Three-Digit Numbers

Write each problem and find the sum.

1.

2.

_____   _____

3. **Number Sense** Matthew wants to show 137 + 429 with place-value blocks. He has enough hundreds and ones blocks, but he only has 4 tens blocks. Can he show the problem? Explain.

_____

4. Museum A has 127 steps. Museum B has 94 steps. Museum C has 108 steps. How many steps do Museums A and B have combined?   _____

5. How many steps do all three museums have?   _____

Test Prep

6. Use the information in Exercise 4. How many steps do Museums A and C have combined?

   A. 254 steps   **B.** 235 steps   **C.** 216 steps   **D.** 188 steps

7. **Writing in Math** Write a number sentence for the place-value blocks below. Find the sum.

   _____

Adding Three-Digit Numbers

Find 237 + 186.

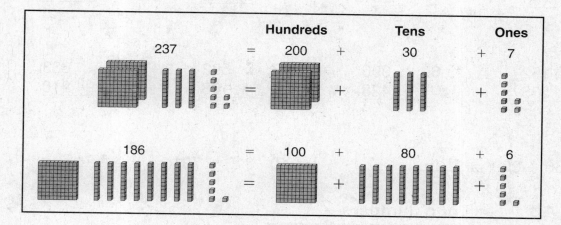

Step 1: Add the ones. 7 ones + 6 ones = 13 ones

Regroup. 13 ones = 1 ten, 3 ones

Step 2: Add the tens. 1 ten + 3 tens + 8 tens = 12 tens

Regroup. 12 tens = 1 hundred, 2 tens

Step 3: Add the hundreds.

1 hundred + 2 hundreds + 1 hundred = 4 hundreds

Add together the hundreds, tens, and ones.

400 + 20 + 3 = 423

1.   118
   + 146

2.   283
   + 147

3.   542
   + 109

4.   220
   + 479

5. Find the sum of 456 and 38.

6. Add 109 and 656.

7. **Estimation** Estimate to decide which sum is less than 600: 356 + 292 or 214 + 356.

Adding Three-Digit Numbers

1. 329
    + 468

2. 148
    + 231

3. 555
    + 777

4. 718
    + 29

5. 152
    + 535

6. 396
    + 428

7. 592
    + 168

8. 633
    + 210

9. 536 + 399 = _____

10. 319 + 791 = _____

Long Jumpers

Animal	Distance (feet)
Flying dragon	100
Flying fish	328
Sugar glider	300

11. What is the total maximum distance that the flying dragon and the flying fish can jump together? _____

12. What is double the sugar glider's maximum gliding distance? _____

Test Prep

13. Find the sum of 163 + 752.

    A. 895   **B.** 915   **C.** 925   **D.** 929

14. **Writing in Math** Write an addition story for two 3-digit numbers. Write the answer to your story.

_____

_____

_____

_____

Adding Three or More Numbers

Find 137 + 201 + 109.

First, estimate. The number 137 is close to 100. The number 201 is close to 200, and the number 109 is close to 100. 100 + 200 + 100 = 400, so the answer should be about 400.

Step 1	Step 2	Step 3	Step 4
Line up the ones, tens, and hundreds.	Add the ones. Regroup as needed.	Add the tens. Regroup as needed.	Add the hundreds.
137 201 + 109	1 137 201 + 109 7	1 137 201 + 109 47	1 137 201 + 109 447
All the numbers are in neat columns so you can add them easily.	Regroup 17 ones into 1 ten and 7 ones.	No need to regroup.	So, 137 + 201 + 109 = 447.

Check to see if the answer is reasonable. Your estimate was 400. 447 is close to 400, so the answer is reasonable.

1. 32
    64
    + 71

2. 127
    39
    + 87

3. 17
    68
    + 32

4. 358
    427
    + 27

5. 382 + 45 + 181 = _____

6. 12 + 138 + 98 = _____

7. **Number Sense** Ranier has 37 baseball cards, 65 football cards, and 151 hockey cards. How many sports cards does he have in all?

_____

Name_____

Adding Three or More Numbers

1.   36
       29
    + 12

2.   142
      297
    + 116

3.   524
       97
    + 190

4.   716
       12
    + 149

5.   156
      561
    + 213

6.   241
      421
    + 124

7.   98
      312
    + 175

8.   420
      318
    + 196

9. **Estimation** Estimate the sum of 327 + 419 + 173. _____

10. **Number Sense** Justine has 162 red buttons, 98 blue buttons, and 284 green buttons. She says she knows she has more than 500 buttons without adding. Do you agree? Explain.

_____

_____

11. Carlos ate 1 oz bran flakes, 1 banana, 1 c whole milk, and 1 c orange juice. How many calories did he eat?

_____

Breakfast

Food	Amount	Calories
Bran flakes	1 oz	90
Banana	1	105
Orange juice	1 c	110
Whole milk	1 c	150

Test Prep

12. Kyle has 378 pennies, 192 nickels, and 117 dimes. How many coins does he have altogether?

    A. 495   **B.** 570   **C.** 677   **D.** 687

13. **Writing in Math** Write an addition problem with 3 addends in which you regroup once to solve.

_____

32 Use with Lesson 3-4.

PROBLEM-SOLVING STRATEGY
Draw a Picture

Fruit Stand Don is selling 18 watermelons. If he sold 7 watermelons in the morning and 6 more during the early afternoon, how many more watermelons could he still sell by the end of the day?

Read and Understand

Step 1: What do you know?

Don is selling 18 watermelons. He has sold 7 in the morning and 6 in the afternoon.

Step 2: What are you trying to find?

How many watermelons Don can still sell by the end of the day

Plan and Solve

What strategy will you use?

Strategy: Draw a picture.

Answer: Don can still sell 5 more watermelons by the end of the day.

Look Back and Check

Is your answer reasonable?

I can see from the picture that 7 + 6 + 5 = 18.

Draw a picture to help you solve the problem, then write the answer.

1. Mike, Bob, and John each gave a balloon to each of the others in the group. How many balloons were given in all?

Name_____

Draw a Picture

Finish the picture for each problem. Write the answer in a complete sentence.

1. Mr. Harper is making a walkway with steppingstones in his garden. He uses a pattern of 1 steppingstone, then 2. How many groups of that pattern can he build with 15 steppingstones?

_____

_____

Draw a picture to solve each problem. Write the answer in a complete sentence.

2. The balloon man at the circus has slippery fingers. Each time he blows up 5 balloons, 3 of them slip from his hands and fly away. How many balloons will he have to blow up before he is holding 8 balloons?

_____

_____

3. Olive's pet cricket jumps 2 in. one day and 3 in. the next. If this pattern continues, how many days will it take Olive's cricket to jump 12 in.?

_____

Regrouping

You can regroup from tens to ones and hundreds to tens by using place-value blocks.

1 ten can be regrouped into 10 ones.

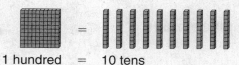

1 ten = 10 ones

1 hundred can be regrouped into 10 tens.

1 hundred = 10 tens

Place-value blocks can also help you to regroup numbers containing hundreds or tens into numbers with tens and ones.

1 hundred gets regrouped into 10 tens.

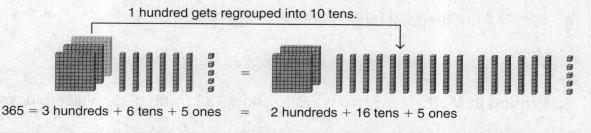

365 = 3 hundreds + 6 tens + 5 ones = 2 hundreds + 16 tens + 5 ones

Regroup 1 ten for 10 ones. You may use place-value blocks or draw a picture to help.

1. 32 = 3̶ _____ tens 2̶ _____ ones   **2.** 47 = 4̶ _____ tens 7̶ _____ ones

Regroup 1 hundred for 10 tens. You may use place-value blocks or draw a picture to help.

3. 176 = 1̶ _____ hundred 7̶ _____ tens 6 ones

4. 243 = 2̶ _____ hundred 4̶ _____ tens 3 ones

5. Number Sense Explain why 249 = 1 hundred, 14 tens, 9 ones.

_____

_____

Regrouping

Regroup 1 ten for 10 ones. You may use place-value blocks
or draw a picture to help.

1. 67 = $\not{6}$ tens, $\not{7}$ ones

67 = _____ tens, _____ ones

2. 30 = $\not{3}$ tens, $\not{0}$ ones

30 = _____ tens, _____ ones

Regroup 1 hundred for 10 tens. You may use place-value
blocks or draw a picture to help.

3. 317 = $\not{3}$ hundreds, $\not{1}$ ten, 7 ones

317 = _____ hundreds, _____ tens, _____ ones

4. 420 = $\not{4}$ hundreds, $\not{2}$ tens, 0 ones

420 = _____ hundreds, _____ tens, _____ ones

5. Writing in Math Draw two ways to show 128 using place-value blocks.

Test Prep

6. 4 hundreds, 2 tens, 17 ones =

A. 4,217   **B.** 427   **C.** 437   **D.** 431

7. Writing in Math Heidi says 381 = 2 hundreds, 7 tens, 11 ones.
Do you agree? Explain.

_____

_____

Subtracting Two-Digit Numbers

Here is how to subtract two-digit numbers.

Find $55 - 36$.

Estimate: $60 - 40 = 20$, so the answer should be about 20.

What You Think	What You Show		What You Write
Step 1 Subtract the ones. Regroup if you need to. Since you can't subtract 6 from 5, regroup.		Regroup 1 ten into 10 ones.	$\begin{array}{r} 4\ 15 \\ 5\!\!\!/5 \\ -36 \\ \hline 9 \end{array}$
		15 ones − 6 ones = 9 ones.	
Step 2 Subtract the tens.		4 tens − 3 tens = 1 ten.	$\begin{array}{r} 4\ 15 \\ 5\!\!\!/5 \\ -36 \\ \hline 19 \end{array}$

Add to check your answer. $19 + 36 = 55$

It checks.

1.
$$\begin{array}{r} 86 \\ -\ 51 \\ \hline \end{array}$$

2.
$$\begin{array}{r} 47 \\ -\ 18 \\ \hline \end{array}$$

3.
$$\begin{array}{r} 62 \\ -\ 35 \\ \hline \end{array}$$

4.
$$\begin{array}{r} 41 \\ -\ 11 \\ \hline \end{array}$$

5. $28 - 17$ _____

6. $53 - 38$ _____

7. **Number Sense** To subtract 91 from 99, do you need to regroup? Explain.

_____

_____

8. Felicia has 67 paperback books in her collection. She sold 48 of them. How many books does she have left?

_____

Subtracting Two-Digit Numbers

1. $\begin{array}{r} 71 \\ -\ 10 \\ \hline \end{array}$ 2. $\begin{array}{r} 65 \\ -\ 18 \\ \hline \end{array}$ 3. $\begin{array}{r} 19 \\ -\ 17 \\ \hline \end{array}$ 4. $\begin{array}{r} 35 \\ -\ 11 \\ \hline \end{array}$

5. $\begin{array}{r} 91 \\ -\ 38 \\ \hline \end{array}$ 6. $\begin{array}{r} 40 \\ -\ 26 \\ \hline \end{array}$ 7. $\begin{array}{r} 21 \\ -\ 17 \\ \hline \end{array}$ 8. $\begin{array}{r} 83 \\ -\ 56 \\ \hline \end{array}$

9. $89 - 66 =$ _____ 10. $52 - 38 =$ _____ 11. $63 - 35 =$ _____

12. Stanton used the addition sentence $21 + 16 = 37$ to check his work. Write two subtraction problems that Stanton could have been checking.

_____

13. The tree farm had 65 shade trees for sale. It sold 39 of the trees. How many trees did it have left?

_____

_____

Test Prep

14. Find the difference of $76 - 38$.

    A. 42   **B.** 38   **C.** 36   **D.** 32

15. **Writing in Math** Bethany has 40 apples. Write a subtraction story about the apples that would require regrouping. Then write the answer in a complete sentence.

_____

_____

_____

_____

Models for Subtracting Three-Digit Numbers

You can use place-value blocks to subtract.

Find 234 − 192.

Estimate: 230 − 190 = 40, so the answer should be about 40.

What You Show		What You Write
Step 1 Show 234 with place-value blocks.		234 −192
Step 2 Subtract the ones. Regroup if needed. 4 > 2. No regrouping is needed.	4 ones − 2 ones = 2 ones	234 −192 2
Step 3 Subtract the tens. Regroup if needed. 3 tens < 9 tens, so regroup 1 hundred for 10 tens.	13 tens − 9 tens = 4 tens	1 13 2̶3̶4 −192 42
Step 4 Subtract the hundreds.	1 hundred − 1 hundred = 0 hundreds	1 13 2̶3̶4 −192 42

Find the value of the remaining blocks:

4 tens + 2 ones = 40 + 2 = 42

So, 234 − 192 = 42.

Find each difference. You may use place-value blocks or draw a picture to help.

1. 156
  − 28

2. 191
  − 122

3. 321
  − 76

4. 446
  − 355

Models for Subtracting Three-Digit Numbers

Find each difference. You may use place-value blocks or draw a picture to help.

1. 321
    − 176

2. 716
    − 99

3. 543
    − 268

4. 133
    − 127

5. 613 − 299 = _____

6. 401 − 102 = _____

7. 836 − 729 = _____

8. 634 − 277 = _____

9. **Number Sense** Tyson wanted to solve 638 − 152.
   He began by finding 6 − 5. Tell what Tyson did wrong.

   _____

   _____

10. What was the difference between the
    greatest and the least number of pages read?

    _____

11. Did Helen read more pages than
    Francis and Lance combined?
    How much more or less did Helen read?

Reading Record	
Name	**Pages Read**
Alexander	716
Carrie	614
Francis	337
Helen	791
Lance	448

Test Prep

12. Simien collected 124 cans for the food drive. Jane collected
    79 cans. How many more cans did Simien collect?

    A. 55   **B.** 52   **C.** 45   **D.** 42

13. **Writing in Math** Write a subtraction sentence in which you
    would have to regroup hundreds.

    _____

Subtracting Three-Digit Numbers

Find 726 − 238.

Estimate: 700 − 200 = 500, so the answer should be about 500.

Step 1	**Step 2**	**Step 3**
First subtract the ones. Regroup if needed.	Subtract the tens. Regroup if needed.	Subtract the hundreds.
1 16 72̸6̸ −238 ___ 8	11 6 1̸ 16 72̸6̸ −238 ___ 88	11 6 1̸ 16 72̸6̸ −238 ___ 488
Regroup 1 ten into 10 ones.	You will need to regroup, since 3 tens > 1 ten. Regroup 1 hundred into 10 tens. This gives you a total of 11 tens.	Is your answer correct? Check by adding: 488 + 238 = 726. It checks.

1. 228
       − 123

2. 291
       − 187

3. 336
       − 275

4. 512
       − 299

5. 175 − 156 = _____

6. 327 − 159 = _____

7. The town library had 634 CDs for rent. During one week, 288 of them were rented. How many CDs were left?   _____

8. Number Sense If you had to subtract 426 from 913, how many times would you need to regroup? How can you tell?

_____

_____

_____

_____

Subtracting Three-Digit Numbers

1. 491 − 216	2. 712 − 328	3. 127 − 35	4. 721 − 153
5. 209 − 16	6. 918 − 436	7. 555 − 164	8. 422 − 244

9. 621 − 411 = _____

10. 318 − 129 = _____

11. 582 − 276 = _____

12. 111 − 89 = _____

13. **Number Sense** Alice found 812 − 413 = 399. She added 812 + 399 to check her work. What did she do wrong?

_____

14. How much taller is the coast redwood than the coast Douglas fir?

_____

Tree Heights

Tree	Height (feet)
Coast redwood	321
Coast Douglas fir	281
Common bald cypress	83

15. What is the difference in height between the coast redwood and the common bald cypress? _____

Test Prep

16. Which is the difference of 811 − 376?

   A. 425   B. 435   C. 436   D. 515

17. **Writing in Math** Kia found the difference of 378 − 299 to be 179. Is she correct? Explain.

_____

_____

Subtracting Across Zero

To subtract from a number with a zero in the tens place, you need to first regroup a hundred into tens.

Find 207 − 98.

Step 1	**Step 2**	**Step 3**
Subtract the ones. Regroup if necessary.	Regroup the hundreds.	Regroup the tens and subtract.
$$\begin{array}{r} 207 \\ -\ 98 \\ \hline \end{array}$$	$$\begin{array}{r} {\scriptstyle 1\ 10} \\ 2\cancel{0}7 \\ -\ 98 \\ \hline \end{array}$$	$$\begin{array}{r} {\scriptstyle 9\ 17} \\ {\scriptstyle 1\ \cancel{10}} \\ 2\cancel{0}7 \\ -\ 98 \\ \hline 109 \end{array}$$
Normally you would regroup 1 ten into 10 ones. Since there are no tens, you must first regroup hundreds.	2 hundreds and 0 tens is equal to 1 hundred and 10 tens. Now you can regroup the tens.	10 tens and 7 ones is the same as 9 tens and 17 ones. Now you can subtract.

1. $\begin{array}{r} 302 \\ -\ 72 \\ \hline \end{array}$ **2.** $\begin{array}{r} 105 \\ -\ 36 \\ \hline \end{array}$ **3.** $\begin{array}{r} 300 \\ -\ 228 \\ \hline \end{array}$ **4.** $\begin{array}{r} 500 \\ -\ 223 \\ \hline \end{array}$

5. 105 − 37 = _____   **6.** 301 − 192 = _____

7. Dave and Chris went bowling. Dave knocked down 300 pins and Chris knocked down 187 pins. How many fewer pins did Chris knock down than Dave? _____

8. Writing in Math Use place-value blocks to draw a picture showing one way to find 406 − 202.

Name_____

Subtracting Across Zero

1. 406
    − 28

2. 300
    − 211

3. 501
    − 268

4. 707
    − 77

5. 605
    − 219

6. 800
    − 579

7. 901
    − 728

8. 704
    − 95

9. 404 − 305 = _____

10. 501 − 223 = _____

11. Patricia estimated that 439 − 186 would be close to 300.
    Do you agree? Explain and solve the problem.

    _____

    _____

12. There are 600 ears of corn for sale at the produce market.
    At the end of the day there are 212 ears left. How many
    ears of corn were sold?

    _____

13. Party Palace has an order for 505 party favors. It packaged 215
    favors in the morning and 180 favors in the afternoon. How
    many party favors does it still need to package to fill the order?

    _____

Test Prep

14. 3 hundreds, 10 tens, 6 ones =

    A. 316   **B.** 306   **C.** 416   **D.** 406

15. **Writing in Math** Explain how you can estimate to tell
    whether 433 − 147 = 286 is reasonable.

    _____

    _____

PROBLEM-SOLVING SKILL   R 3-11

Exact Answer or Estimate?

There are times when an estimate is enough to solve a problem.
Sometimes an exact answer is needed.

Reading Competition Sanjay and Teresa
are having a reading competition. The
table shows how many books each
has read. How many more books has
Sanjay read than Teresa?

Month	Sanjay	Teresa
January	12 books	15 books
February	27 books	21 books
March	22 books	8 books
April	6 books	13 books

The problem asks for an exact answer.
To find out the exact answer, you need
to add the books read by Sanjay and the books read by Teresa.
Sanjay read 67 books. Teresa read 57 books. Then you need to
subtract the number of books read by Teresa from the number
of books read by Sanjay. $67 - 57 = 10$. Sanjay read exactly
10 more books than Teresa.

If the question had been "Who has read more books, Sanjay or
Teresa?" an estimate would be enough.

Water Park Crowd On a sunny day, 108 people were at the water
park. After an hour, 36 people had left. A little bit later, 24 people came
back to the water park. How many people are now at the water park?

1. What operations will you use? Explain.

   _____

   _____

2. Is an estimate enough? Explain.

   _____

   _____

3. Solve the problem. Write your answer in a complete sentence.

   _____

   _____

PROBLEM-SOLVING SKILL

Exact Answer or Estimate?

Were less than 50 sack lunches eaten
during the week?

Sack Lunches	
Monday:	▢ ▢ ▢ ▢
Tuesday:	▢
Wednesday:	▢ ▢ ▢ ▢ ▢
Thursday:	▢ ▢ ▢
Friday:	▢ ▢ ◹
Each ▢ = 2 sack lunches.	
Each ◹ = 1 sack lunch.	

1. What do you know?

   _____

   _____

   _____

2. What are you trying to find?

   _____

   _____

3. What operation will you use? _____

4. Is an estimate enough? Explain.

   _____

   _____

   _____

5. Solve the problem. Give your answer in a complete sentence.

   _____

   _____

6. How many more sack lunches were eaten on Wednesday
   than on Thursday?

   _____

Adding and Subtracting Money

Find $12.50 + $9.25.

Estimate: $13 + $9 = $22.

Step 1	**Step 2**
Add as you would with whole numbers. Make sure to line up the decimal points before adding.	Write the answer in dollars and cents. Be sure to include the decimal point.

<table>
<tr><td>

```
     1
  $12.50
+    9.25
  21 75
```
</td><td>

```
     1
  $12.50
+    9.25
  $21.75
```
</td></tr>
</table>

$12.50 + $9.25 = $21.75

1.
```
  $2.87
+  1.09
```

2.
```
  $15.31
−   2.27
```

3.
```
  $ 3.67
+  13.22
```

4.
```
  $10.07
−   0.88
```

5. $7.65 + $0.82 _____

6. $17.21 − $12.33 _____

7. $14.31 + $36.29 _____

8. $9.27 − $8.85 _____

9. Wallace bought a model airplane for $6.93.
He paid with a $20 bill. How much change did
Wallace get back?   _____

10. Writing in Math Samina wants to pay for some balloons
with a $10 bill. The balloons cost $1.79. Samina estimates
that she will get $7.00 back in change. Do you agree with
her estimate? Explain.

_____

_____

_____

Name_____

Adding and Subtracting Money

1. $$7.29
    $- \quad 1.03$

2. $3.50
    $+ \quad 2.91$

3. $6.00
    $- \quad 2.59$

4. $17.99
    $- \quad 13.86$

5. $20.00
    $- \quad 18.42$

6. $12.04
    $+ \quad 3.16$

7. $4.21
    $+ \quad 3.99$

8. $6.18
    $- \quad 3.19$

9. $7.83 + $0.62 = _____

10. $16.02 − $5.19 = _____

11. $18.21 + $14.36 = _____

12. $27.36 − $15.29 = _____

13. Liz gets paid $4.75 each day for delivering newspapers. How much money will she have after delivering newspapers for 3 days?

_____

14. Liz saved her money for 3 days to buy new tennis shoes for $16.98. Tell how much money she still needs or how much she will have left over.

_____

Test Prep

15. Sam paid for a notebook that costs $0.76 with a $1.00 bill. What was his change?

    A. $0.24   **B.** $0.42   **C.** $0.75   **D.** $0.34

16. **Writing in Math** Austin paid for $4.77 worth of groceries with a $5.00 bill. Could he have received a quarter with his change? Explain.

_____

_____

_____

Name_____

Choose a Computation Method

R 3-13

Use mental math to solve problems that are simple.

Example: 250 + 200

Use paper and pencil, and make estimates to solve problems
with two or more regroupings.

Example: 524 + 217
I estimate 524 to be 500. I estimate 217
to be 200. So, my answer should be about 700.
My estimate of 700 is close to 741.

```
  1
  524
+ 217
  741
```

Use a calculator to solve problems with many regroupings.
Example: 23,142 − 17,565
First I'll estimate by rounding to the nearest thousand:
23,000 − 18,000 = 6,000.
23,142 − 17,565 = 5,577

My estimate of 6,000 is close to 5,577.

Use mental math, paper and pencil, or a calculator to solve.

1.	2.	3.	4.
1,200 + 800	$26.91 + 42.03	300 − 109	96,346 − 18,982

5. Backbone Mountain in Maryland is 3,360 ft high. Mount
Washington in New Hampshire is 6,288 ft high. How much
higher is Mount Washington than Backbone Mountain?
Write your answer in a complete sentence.

_____

_____

_____

© Pearson Education, Inc. 3

Choose a Computation Method

Use mental math, paper and pencil, or a calculator to solve.

1. $716 - 310$

2. $11,234 - 2,378$

3. $\$4.76 + 2.25$

4. $720 - 319$

5. $\$32.61 + 19.86$

6. $780 - 298$

7. $400 - 312$

8. $204,516 + 307,629$

9. $158 + 269 =$ _____

10. $\$13.00 - \$9.57 =$ _____

11. **Number Sense** Would you use mental math to solve $2,984 + 1,997 + 406$? Explain.

_____

_____

12. Pauline subtracted $3,162 - 1,498$ as shown.

    What did Pauline do wrong?

    $\begin{array}{r} 3,162 \\ -1,498 \\ \hline 2,664 \end{array}$

_____

_____

Test Prep

13. Find $650 - 298$.

    A. 352   **B.** 350   **C.** 302   **D.** 358

14. **Writing in Math** Solve this problem with pencil and paper: $2,593 + 1,389$. Tell one way you could check your answer.

_____

_____

Equality and Inequality

A number sentence that uses < (less than) or > (greater than) is an inequality. Example: 8 > 1 + 6. This equation is read as 8 is *greater than* 1 + 6.

You can add or subtract on each side of a number sentence to decide if the sentence is true or false.

9 + 7 > 8 + 6

16 > 14

True

9 − 2 > 8 + 1

7 > 9

False

Find a number to make the number sentence true.

3 + _____ > 8

Try 2.   3 + 2 > 8

5 > 8 False

Try 7.   3 + 7 > 8

10 > 8 True

Compare. Write <, >, or = for each ◯.

1. 13 + 7 ◯ 20

2. 14 + 22 ◯ 37 + 1

3. 42 − 18 ◯ 27 + 6

4. 28 − 14 ◯ 5 + 9

Find three whole numbers that make each number sentence true.

5. 5 + _____ < 15

_____

6. 19 − _____ < 12

_____

7. 27 + _____ > 30

_____

Equality and Inequality

Compare. Write <, >, or = for each $\bigcirc$.

1. 20 $\bigcirc$ 13 + 9

2. 14 − 7 $\bigcirc$ 16 − 8

3. 32 + 5 + 3 $\bigcirc$ 40

4. 268 − 112 $\bigcirc$ 112 + 268

5. $3.29 + $7.16 $\bigcirc$ $10.50

6. 1 + 2 + 3 $\bigcirc$ 3 + 2 + 1

Find three whole numbers that make each number sentence true.

7. 15 + x > 18   x = _____

8. 375 − n < 200   n = _____

9. Which two animals are able to spend an equal number of minutes under water?

_____

_____

Average Breath-Holding Time Underwater

Animal	Minutes
Hippopotamus	15
Muskrat	12
Platypus	10
Porpoise	15
Sea otter	5

10. The muskrat can hold its breath for a greater amount of time than which two animals?

_____

Test Prep

11. Which number does not make the number sentence

26 + y > 30 true?

A. 10   **B.** 4   **C.** 7   **D.** 100

12. **Writing in Math** Write a number sentence with two expressions that equal each other.

_____

_____

Name_____

Small Countries

This chart shows the area of several small countries.

If Grenada's area was increased by 84 square kilometers, how many square kilometers would it be?

Land Areas

Country	Area (square kilometers)
Monaco	2
Nauru	21
San Marino	60
Marshall Islands	181
Maldives	300
Malta	321
Grenada	339

Step 1

Add the ones.
Regroup.
13 ones = 1 ten, 3 ones

```
  1
 339
+ 84
   3
```

Step 2

Add the tens.
Regroup.
12 tens = 1 hundred, 2 tens

```
 11
 339
+ 84
  23
```

Step 3

Add the hundreds.

```
 11
 339
+ 84
 423
```

$339 + 84 = 423$

Grenada would be 423 square kilometers.

1. What is the area of Nauru and San Marino combined? _____

2. What is the area of the Marshall Islands and Maldives combined? _____

3. How much larger is Malta than Nauru? _____

4. How much smaller is San Marino than Grenada? _____

5. What is the area of Malta, Maldives, and the Marshall Islands combined? _____

Name_____

Bow-Wow Facts

The American Kennel Club (AKC) is a national group that has lots of information about dogs, including ways to keep dogs healthy, facts about different kinds of dogs, and rules in dog shows.

1. The AKC says that a male Alaskan malamute show dog should weigh about 85 lb and that a female should weigh about 10 lb less. About how much should a female weigh?

_____

2. The average female St. Bernard show dog weighs about 145 lb. The average male St. Bernard weighs about 20 lb more. About how much does the average male St. Bernard show dog weigh?

_____

3. Suppose you have 3 greyhounds for pets. They weigh 56 lb, 72 lb, and 63 lb. What is their combined weight?

_____

4. Suppose you want to buy some 40 lb bags of dog food at $33.00 per bag, including tax. If you had $100.00, could you buy 3 bags? Explain.

_____

_____

5. Suppose you wanted to buy some dog toys and supplies. The total cost is $127.73. To find how much change you would get from $150.00, would it be best to use mental math, pencil and paper, or a calculator? Explain.

_____

_____

Time to the Half Hour and Quarter Hour

Time can be measured in half hours and quarter hours.

30 minutes = 1 half hour

15 minutes = 1 quarter hour

The hours of a day are divided into A.M. and P.M. hours. A.M. hours begin at 12 midnight and end at 12 noon. P.M. hours begin at 12 noon and end at 12 midnight.

The clocks show the times of three events that happen every day at an elementary school.

Reading	Lunch	Recess

What you write: 9:30   12:15

Here are different ways to say each time.

9:30   **nine thirty** or **half past nine**

12:15   **twelve fifteen** or **fifteen minutes after twelve** or **quarter after twelve**

1:45   **one forty-five** or **fifteen minutes to two** or **quarter to two**

Write the time shown on each clock in two ways.

1.   7:15   _____

                             _____

2.    _____

                             _____

Name_____

Time to the Half Hour and Quarter Hour

Write the time shown on each clock in two ways.

1.

   _____

   _____

2.

   _____

   _____

3. **Number Sense** Would it take closer to a minute
   or an hour to clean your room? _____

4. The school bus stops at Randy's bus stop at 8:15 A.M.
   Randy arrived at the bus stop at a quarter after 8:00. Did
   he miss the bus? Explain.

   _____

   _____

Test Prep

5. Which does NOT describe 5:15?

   A. five forty-five   **B.** quarter after five

   C. five fifteen   **D.** fifteen minutes after five

6. **Writing in Math** Explain the difference between A.M. and P.M.

   _____

   _____

   _____

Name_____

Time to the Minute

You can skip count by fives and then count on to tell time when the minute hand is between numbers.

The minute hand is between 7 and 8.

Count by 5s from 12 to 7. That is 35 minutes.

Count 3 more minutes. There are 38 minutes.

The hour hand is between 11 and 12. The time is 11:38, or 22 minutes to 12.

Write the time shown on each clock two ways.

1.

_____

_____

2.

_____

_____

3.

_____

_____

Name_____

Time to the Minute

Write the time shown on each clock two ways.

1.

_____

_____

2.

_____

_____

3. **Number Sense** If Patricia won the race, who finished last?

_____

4. **Reasoning** Who finished closest to 8:00 P.M.?

_____

Marathon Run

Runner	Finish Time
Abbot, Frank	7:55 P.M.
Darling, Jasper	12:18 A.M.
Lawston, Ceilia	10:32 P.M.
Olson, Patricia	6:17 P.M.
Volst, Sandra	8:19 P.M.

5. Did Ceilia Lawston finish before or after 10:40 P.M.?

_____

Test Prep

6. Jan's alarm clock goes off at 12 minutes before 7:00 A.M. How many minutes past 6:00 A.M. is that?

   A. 48   **B.** 21   **C.** 19   **D.** 12

7. **Writing in Math** Write the time you are finished with school each day in two ways.

_____

Name_____

Elapsed Time

A children's museum is open from 1:00 P.M. to 6:35 P.M. every day. How long is the museum open?

Step 1	**Step 2**	**Step 3**
Find the starting time.	Count the hours.	Count the minutes.

Start at 1:00.

There are 5 hours from 1:00 P.M. to 6:00 P.M.

There are 35 minutes from 6:00 to 6:35. The time elapsed is 5:35.

Find the elapsed time.

1. **Start time:** 8:00 A.M.
   End time: 1:15 P.M.
   _____

2. **Start time:** 3:25 A.M.
   End time: 5:40 A.M.
   _____

3. **Start time:** 12:00 P.M.
   End time: 3:48 P.M.
   _____

4. **Number Sense** A science class lasted from 1:15 until 2:05. Did the science class last more than or less than 1 hr?

   _____

Name_____

Elapsed Time

Find the elapsed time.

1. Start Time: 6:00 P.M.
   End Time: 7:15 P.M.

   _____

2. Start Time: 9:30 A.M.
   End Time: 11:55 A.M.

   _____

3. Start Time: 4:15 P.M.
   End Time: 7:22 P.M.

   _____

4. Start Time: 3:48 P.M.
   End Time: 8:11 P.M.

   _____

5. Tara's baby sister naps between 12:45 P.M. and 2:30 P.M. every
   day. How long is the baby's nap?

   _____

6. Write the beginning time and the ending time of your
   school day. What is the elapsed time of your school day?

   _____

   _____

Test Prep

7. Which is the elapsed time?   Start Time: 1:01 P.M.
                                End Time: 3:02 P.M.

   A. 3 hr 1 min   B. 2 hr 12 min

   C. 2 hr 2 min   D. 2 hr 1 min

8. **Writing in Math** Would you rather have your recess last
   from 10:30 A.M. to 10:45 A.M. or from 10:45 A.M. to
   11:10 A.M.? Explain.

   _____

   _____

   _____

Using a Calendar

You can use a calendar to find the days of the week and the months of a year.

Time	Order of the Months
1 week = 7 days	January
52 weeks = 1 year	February
	March
1 year = 12 months	April
	May
1 year = 365 days	June
	July
1 leap year = 366 days	August
	September
1 decade = 10 years	October
	November
1 century = 100 years	December

November

S	M	T	W	T	F	S
						1
2	3	4	5	6	7	8
9	10	11	12	13	14	15
16	17	18	19	20	21	22
23	24	25	26	27	28	29
30						

What is the ninth month of the year?
  Count nine months starting with January. September is the ninth month of the year.

What date is the second Tuesday in November?
  Locate the Tuesday column on the calendar. The 4th is the first Tuesday, and the 11th is the second Tuesday.

1. How many Mondays were there in November? _____

2. What date was the fourth Friday in November? _____

3. How many Sundays were there in November? _____

4. What day of the week was November 12? _____

5. **Number Sense** About how many days are there in two months?

   _____

6. Write the ordinal number that represents the month of November when the months of the year are listed in order. _____

7. **Number Sense** How many weeks are in two years? _____

Name_____

Using a Calendar

1. Write the ordinal number for the month of March. _____

2. **Number Sense** How many months are in two years? _____

Use the calendar for Exercises 3–7.

3. How many Sundays were in June?

_____

June 2002

S	M	T	W	T	F	S
						1
2	3	4	5	6	7	8
9	10	11	12	13	14	15
16	17	18	19	20	21	22
23	24	25	26	27	28	29
30						

4. What day of the week was June 1?

_____

5. Miguel left for vacation June 11. He returned home June 25. How many weeks was he gone? _____

6. **Reasoning** On what day of the week was the Fourth of July celebrated? _____

7. Mr. Evans began to paint his house on June 14. It takes him nine days to finish the job. On what date did he finish painting the house? _____

Test Prep

8. Macy's piano lessons begin the 1st of September. She has lessons for eight months. Which is the last month of her piano lessons?

    A. March   **B.** April   **C.** June   **D.** July

9. **Writing in Math** Do some people live eight centuries or eight decades? Explain.

_____

_____

_____

Using Tally Charts to Organize Data   R 4-5

Students were asked, "What is your favorite subject at school?"
You can use tally charts to help you organize data you collect
from the survey.

Each subject that students chose as their favorite was listed,
and a tally mark was recorded for each time that subject was
given as an answer.

Period	Tally Marks	Number
Reading	ⅢⅡ II	7
Math	ⅢⅡ ⅢⅡ I	11
Science	IIII	4
Gym	ⅢⅡ I	6

1. What is the most popular subject in the survey?   _____

2. How many students answered the survey altogether?   _____

3. In the survey, what is the least popular subject?   _____

4. **Number Sense** What number is shown by

    ⅢⅡ ⅢⅡ IIII   _____

Use the data at the right for 5–7.

5. Make a tally chart to show the results.

Favorite Animal			
Lion	Duck	Lion	Tiger
Bear	Tiger	Bear	Lion
Bear	Lion	Tiger	Tiger
Tiger	Lion	Duck	Bear

6. How many people voted?   _____

7. Which animals got the same number of votes?

_____

Using Tally Charts to Organize Data

Phillip took a survey to find out the age of each person in his class.

Ages of Classmates

Age	Tally	Number
8 years	卌 I	6
9 years	卌 卌 II	12
10 years	III	3

1. How old are most of Phillip's classmates? _____

2. How many students are in Phillip's class? _____

3. How many more students are 8 years old than 10 years old? _____

4. There are twice as many 9-year-olds than what age group? _____

5. Are there more or fewer students in Phillip's class than in your class?

_____

_____

Test Prep

6. Which shows the number for 卌 卌 卌 卌 IIII?

   A. 14   B. 24   C. 25   D. 44

7. **Writing in Math** Name five different topics that can be used to take a survey.

_____

_____

_____

Using Line Plots to Organize Data

This line plot shows the size in centimeters of a group of caterpillars. Each X represents one caterpillar.

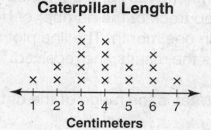

Caterpillar Length

To find the range of this set of data, you subtract the least number from the greatest number. $7 - 1 = 6$, so the range of the data is 6.

To find the mode of this set of data, you look to see which centimeter measure appears most often on the line plot. Three centimeters has the most Xs above it, so the mode of the data is 3 cm.

A group of third graders sold tomato plants to help buy a new flagpole for the school. The number of tomato plants students sold is shown on the line plot. Use the line plot to answer 1–6. Each X represents one student.

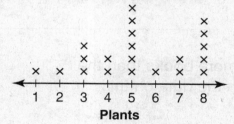

Number of Plants Sold

1. What is the mode of this data?   _____

2. How many students sold exactly five plants each?   _____

3. How many students sold exactly six plants?   _____

4. How many students sold fewer than five plants each? _____

5. What is the range of this data?   _____

6. **Reasoning** Two students sold exactly the same number of plants. How many could they have sold? List all of the possible answers.   _____

Name_____

Using Line Plots to Organize Data

Ms. Temple, the librarian, asked students to keep track of the number of books they read in one month. The line plot at the right shows the results she received.

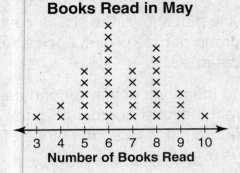

Books Read in May

Number of Books Read

1. What is the range of the data?

   _____

2. How many students kept track of their reading for Ms. Temple?

   _____

3. How many students read 7 books?

   _____

4. How many fewer students read 8 books than 6 books?

   _____

5. How many books were read by 3 of the students?

   _____

6. What is the mode for the data?

   _____

7. **Reasoning** Janice says the girls read more books than the boys. Can she prove her statement with the data on this line plot? Explain.

   _____

   _____

Test Prep

8. Which of the following is the difference between the greatest and the least numbers in the data?

   A. Mode   **B.** Median   **C.** Mean   **D.** Range

9. **Writing in Math** Phyllis says you can plot favorite colors of a sixth-grade class on a line plot. Do you agree? Explain.

   _____

   _____

Reading Pictographs and Bar Graphs

Pictographs use pictures or parts of pictures to represent data.
Bar graphs use bars to represent data.

| **Pictographs** | **Bar Graphs** |

Gold Medals Won at 1998 Winter Olympics

Japan	🏅 🏅 🏅 🏅 🏅
Italy	🏅 🏅
Canada	🏅 🏅 🏅 🏅 🏅 🏅
Korea	🏅 🏅 🏅

Each 🏅 stands for 1 gold medal.

Japan won __5__ gold medals.

Canada won __6__ gold medals.

2000 Summer Olympics

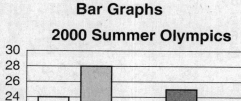

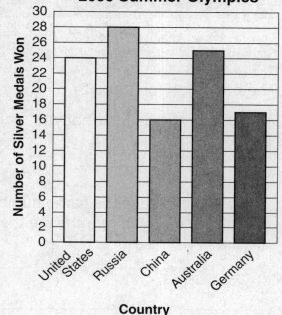

_____ won 28 silver medals in 2000.

Germany won _____ silver medals in 2000.

---

1. How many houses were built in City B in 2002?

   _____

2. How many houses were built in City A in 2002?

   _____

Number of Houses Built in 2002

City A	🏠 🏠 🏠 🏠 🏠
City B	🏠 🏠 🏠 🏠
City C	🏠 🏠 🏠 🏠
City D	🏠 🏠 🏠 🏠 🏠 🏠 🏠

Each 🏠 = 10 houses.
Each 🏠 = 5 houses.

Reading Pictographs and Bar Graphs   **P 4-7**

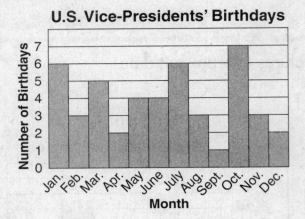

U.S. Vice-Presidents' Birthdays

U.S. Presidents' Birthdays

January	🚶🚶
February	🚶🚶
March	🚶🚶🚶
April	🚶🚶
May	🚶
June	🚶
July	🚶🚶
August	🚶🚶
September	🚶
October	🚶🚶🚶
November	🚶🚶🚶
December	🚶🚶

Key

Each 🚶 stands for 2 presidents.

Use the bar graph for 1 and 2.

1. Which month has 5 birthdays?

_____

2. Three months have the same number of birthdays. Which months are they?

_____

_____

Use the pictograph for 3 and 4.

3. How many months have the birthdays of 4 presidents?

_____

4. **Number Sense** If August had 3 more figures, how many birthdays would be represented?

_____

Test Prep

5. Which of the following do pictographs and bar graphs represent?

   A. Ideas   **B.** Directions   **C.** Data   **D.** Estimation

6. **Writing in Math** Look at both of the graphs above. What do you notice about the number of birthdays during October as compared to the number of birthdays during any other month?

_____

50   Use with Lesson 4-7.

PROBLEM-SOLVING SKILL
Writing to Compare

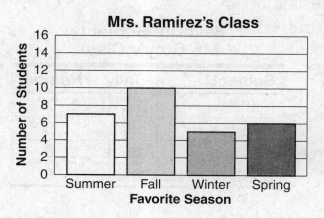

Mrs. Ramirez's Class

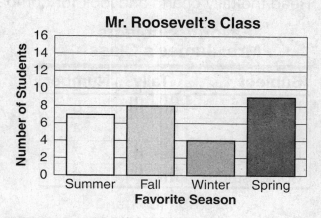

Mr. Roosevelt's Class

Question	Comparison Statements	Tips for Writing Good Comparisons
How are the groups alike?	Winter is the least favorite season for both groups. Summer had the same number of votes for both groups.	Use comparison words such as *most*, *least*, and *about the same*.
How are the groups different?	Fall had the greatest number of votes in Mrs. Ramirez's class, but spring had the greatest number of votes in Mr. Roosevelt's class.	Use contrast words such as *but* or *however*.

Bill's Sports Card Collections

Baseball	☐
Football	☐ ☐ ☐ ☐ ☐
Hockey	☐ ☐ ☐ ☐ ▯
Basketball	☐ ☐ ☐ ☐ ☐

Each ☐ = 10 cards.

Terry's Sports Card Collections

Baseball	☐ ▯
Football	☐ ☐ ☐ ☐ ☐ ☐ ☐
Hockey	☐
Basketball	☐ ☐

Each ☐ = 10 cards.

1. Write a statement about how Bill and Terry's collections are alike.

_____

2. Write a statement about how Bill and Terry's collections are different.

_____

Name_____

PROBLEM-SOLVING SKILL
Writing to Compare

Read the tally charts and look for comparisons.

**Favorite Subjects
Mrs. James's Class**

Subject	Tally	Number
Math	ℍℍ III	8
Science	IIII	4
Reading	ℍℍ II	7
Social studies	ℍℍ I	6

**Favorite Subjects
Mr. Grey's Class**

Subject	Tally	Number
Math	ℍℍ II	7
Science	ℍℍ	5
Reading	ℍℍ I	6
Social studies	ℍℍ I	6

1. Write two statements that compare the favorite subjects of the students in the two classes.

_____

_____

_____

_____

2. Two students were absent from school the day Mr. Grey's class took this survey. How many students does Mr. Grey teach?

_____

3. Two students in Mrs. James's class chose music and one student chose art. How many students are in Mrs. James's class?

_____

4. **Writing in Math** How can graphs and charts help us make comparisons?

_____

_____

_____

_____

Graphing Ordered Pairs

The Amusement Park

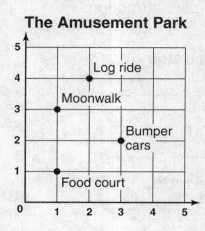

How to Name a Point

The bumper cars are at point (3, 2) on the grid. Start at (0, 0). Move 3 places to the right and 2 places up. (3, 2) is called an ordered pair.

The moonwalk is at (1, 3). The log ride is at (2, 4).

How to Locate a Point

What is located at (1, 1)?
Move 1 space to the right and 1 space up.
You are at the food court. It is at (1, 1).

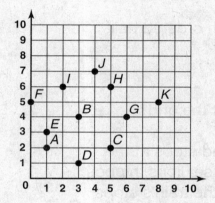

Write the ordered pair that describes the location of each point.

1. A _____   **2.** B _____

3. C _____   **4.** D _____

Give the letter of the point named by each ordered pair.

5. (0, 5) _____   **6.** (8, 5) _____

7. (1, 3) _____   **8.** (6, 4) _____

9. Writing in Math Describe the difference between locating a point at (1, 3) and a point at (3, 1).

_____

_____

Name_____

Graphing Ordered Pairs

Write the ordered pair that describes the location of each attraction.

1. Elephants

_____

2. Train station

_____

3. Hippos

_____

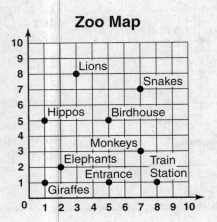

Zoo Map

Give the name of the attraction located by each ordered pair.

4. (3, 8) _____   **5.** (7, 3) _____

6. Which attraction is closest to the center of the grid? _____

7. The train ride begins at the train station and stops at the attractions in this order: monkeys, birdhouse, lions, hippos, and elephants. Write the ordered pairs of the train's stops in order.

_____

Test Prep

8. Which point is at (7, 2)?

A. *A*

B. *B*

C. *C*

D. *D*

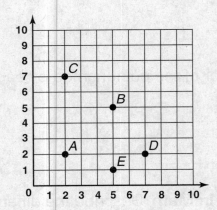

9. Writing in Math Cooper says the ordered pair for point *E* on the grid above is (1, 5). Do you agree? Explain.

_____

Name_____

Reading Line Graphs

How can you find out how much rain fell at 1 P.M. on Monday?

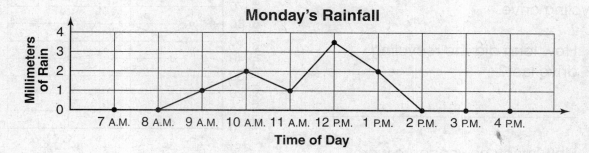

Monday's Rainfall

Step 1 Find the point for 1 P.M. Move your finger along the bottom of the graph until you find 1 P.M.

Step 2 Move your finger up until you reach the point.

Step 3 Find the number on the left of the graph that matches the point. Read the number on the scale. The point is at 2 mm.

At 1 P.M., 2 mm of rain fell.

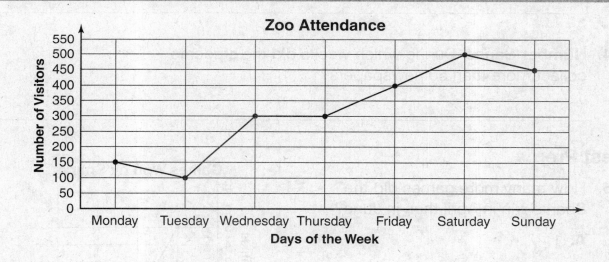

Zoo Attendance

1. How many people visited the zoo on Monday? _____

2. How many days did less than 350 people visit the zoo? _____

3. **Reasoning** Is it correct to say that the zoo was the most crowded on the weekend? Explain.

_____

_____

Reading Line Graphs

The students in Mr. Blake's room collected newspapers for the recycling drive.

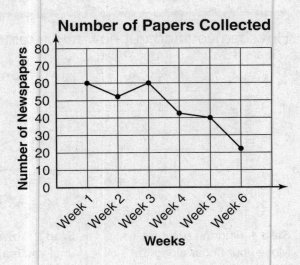

Number of Papers Collected

1. How long did the recycling drive last?

   _____

2. How many newspapers were collected the first week?

   _____

3. What happened to the number of newspapers after the third week?

   _____

4. **Number Sense** During which weeks did the students collect more than 50 newspapers?

   _____

Test Prep

5. How many more games did the Sharks win in April than in June?

   A. 1

   B. 2

   C. 3

   D. 4

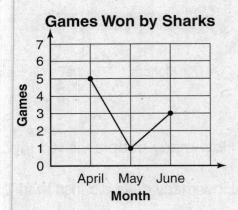

Games Won by Sharks

6. **Writing in Math** How does a line graph make it easy to see changes over time?

   _____

   _____

Making Pictographs

A restaurant kept track of the number of items it sold in one hour. The tally table shows how many of each item was ordered. Use this data to make a pictograph.

Food	Tally	Number
Pasta	ЖЖ I	6
Salad	IIII	4
Casserole	ЖЖ ЖЖ	10
Fish	ЖЖ III	8

_____

Pasta	
Salad	
Casserole	
Fish	

Each ____ = ____ meals.

Step 1 Write a title to explain what the pictograph shows.

Step 2 Choose a symbol for the key. Because this pictograph is about food, a fork might be a good symbol. Add your symbol to the key. Decide how many votes each fork will stand for. Add this to the key.

Step 3 Decide how many symbols are needed for each food. Draw them.

The data below show how Ms. Hashimoto's class voted on their favorite types of videos to rent.

Favorite Video	Tally	Number
Action	ЖЖ III	
Comedy	III	
Drama	ЖЖ I	
Animated	ЖЖ ЖЖ	

Action	
Comedy	
Drama	
Animated	

Each [☐] = ____ votes.

1. Complete the table.

2. Complete the pictograph.

3. **Writing in Math** Write a title for the table and pictograph above.

Making Pictographs

Sanchez made an organized list of the marbles in his marble collection.

My Marbles	
Blue	16
Red	24
Green	28
Yellow	14
Metallic	4

1. Use Sanchez's list to complete the pictograph.

Sanchez's Marbles

Blue	
Red	
Green	
Yellow	
Metallic	

Key Each _____ = _____ marbles.

2. Which type of marble would you say Sanchez would consider rare? Explain.

_____

_____

Test Prep

3. Where can you look to find out what each symbol stands for on a pictograph?

A. Title   **B.** Key   **C.** Data   **D.** Symbol

4. **Writing in Math** Pamela made a pictograph showing students' favorite drinks. Pamela drew 3 glasses to represent the 6 students who chose chocolate milk. Is her pictograph right? Explain.

Favorite Drinks

Drink	Number of Students
Chocolate milk	⬜ ⬜ ⬜
Fruit juice	⬜ ⬜ ⬜ ⬜

Key Each ⬜ = 2 students.

_____

Making Bar Graphs

The table shows the number of different kinds of birds that visited a bird feeder over five days.

Day	Number of Birds
Monday	6
Tuesday	4
Wednesday	7
Thursday	5
Friday	3

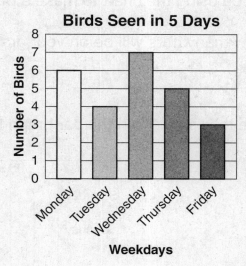

Birds Seen in 5 Days

How to make a bar graph:

Step 1 Label the bottom of the graph "Weekdays" and name the 5 weekdays that will be below the bars.

Step 2 Number the scale from 0 to 8 to show the number of birds. Label the scale "Number of Birds."

Step 3 Make bars for the days of the week shown in the table.

Step 4 Give the graph a title.

You will be using the table below to finish a bar graph.

Record Fish

Type of Fish	Weight of Largest One Caught
Bull trout	32 lb
Black skipjack	26 lb
Pollock	50 lb
Channel catfish	58 lb

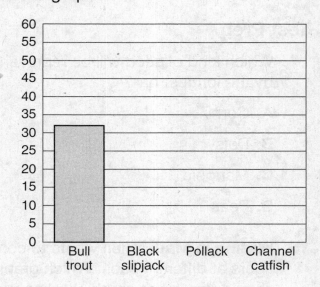

1. Complete the bar graph by drawing the rest of the bars. Insert labels and give your graph a title.

Name_____

Making Bar Graphs

The table shows the number of phone calls
Mrs. Walker made during five days of fundraising.
You will be using the chart to make a bar graph.

Fundraising Calls

Day	Phone Calls
Saturday	26
Sunday	19
Monday	20
Tuesday	24
Wednesday	16

1. How many bars will be on your graph?

_____

2. Use the list to finish the bar graph that Mrs. Walker started.

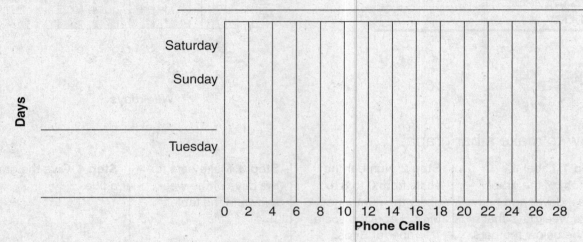

3. How many calls did Mrs. Walker make on
   the weekend?   _____

Test Prep

4. Which kind of seed will be represented
   by the longest bar?

   A. Corn

   B. Daisy

   C. Marigold

   D. Peas

Seed	Sprouts
Corn	13
Daisy	7
Marigold	5
Peas	15

5. **Writing in Math** Allen wants to compare the numbers of
   tigers at different zoos. Which graph do you think he
   should use, a bar graph or a line graph? Explain.

_____

Name_____

Making Line Graphs

R 4-13

The table shows the number of garbage cans emptied by a truck for four days. Make a line graph to show how the number changed from day to day.

Garbage Cans Emptied

Day	Number of Cans
1	20
2	40
3	30
4	15

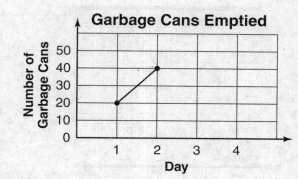

On the third day, 30 cans were emptied. Find the 3 at the bottom of the graph and 30 along the side. Draw a point at the place where 3 and 30 meet. Draw a line to connect that point with the point for the second day.

Plot the point for the fourth day and draw a line to connect it to the third day.

Days Temperature Below 20°F

Month	Number of Days
January	12
February	8
March	6

1. Use the data in the chart to complete the line graph that has been started to the right.

2. Is the number of days below 20°F increasing or decreasing each month?

_____

© Pearson Education, Inc. 3

56 Use with Lesson 4-13.

Making Line Graphs

Anson kept track of how tall his sunflower was each week. His organized list is shown.

Height of Sunflower

Week	Inches
1	$\frac{1}{2}$
2	1
3	4
4	$8\frac{1}{2}$
5	13

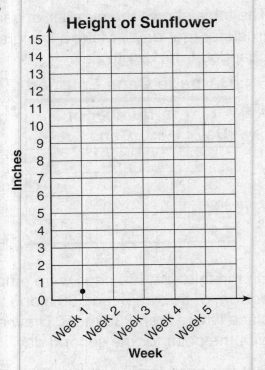

1. Use the data to finish the line graph.

2. How much did Anson's sunflower grow from Week 2 to Week 3?

_____

3. **Reasoning** What do you think will happen during Week 6?

_____

_____

Test Prep

4. How many more books did Sasha read in April than in February?

   A. 2   **B.** 4

   C. 5   **D.** 7

5. **Writing in Math** Describe the difference between the number of books Sasha read in April and in May.

_____

_____

PROBLEM-SOLVING STRATEGY

Make a Graph

Rainy Days Allison kept track of the number of rainy days for 5 months. How did the number of rainy days change over 5 months?

Month	Number of Rainy Days
April	10
May	7
June	3
July	7
August	5

Read and Understand

Step 1: What do you know?

I know the number of rainy days for 5 months.

Step 2: What are you trying to find?

I need to know how the number of rainy days changed over 5 months.

Plan and Solve

Step 3: What strategy will you use?

- I will enter all known data and look for a pattern.
- I will read the graph to answer the question.

Answer: There were 2 months when the number of rainy days was 7. June had the least number of rainy days. April had the most.

Strategy: Make a graph.

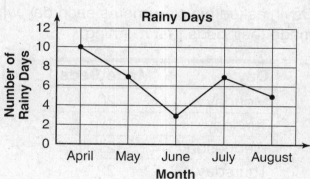

Look Back and Check

Is your work correct?

Yes, the graph shows the correct data.

1. Complete the pictograph.
Use the data in the chart.

Sports Played by 3rd Graders

Sport	Number of Students
Softball	7
Hockey	14
Baseball	6
Tennis	8

Sports Played by 3rd Graders

Sport	Number of Students
Softball	
Hockey	
Baseball	
Tennis	

Each 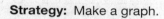 = 2 students.

Name_____

Make a Graph

Ashley asked each person in her class
how many televisions their family owned.

Solve. Write your answer in a complete sentence.

Number of Televisions Owned

1. Complete the graph using the data.

Number of Televisions Owned						
0	5	2	1	2	3	4
2	4	3	2	3	1	1
1	1	2	3	3	0	2

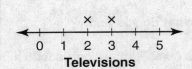

Televisions

2. Which number of televisions is most common?

_____

Devin asked his classmates each day whether or not they
made their beds that morning.

Day	Made Beds
Monday	20
Tuesday	17
Wednesday	21
Thursday	22
Friday	19

3. Complete the bar graph using the
   data above.

4. On which day did Devin's classmates
   make their beds the least?

_____

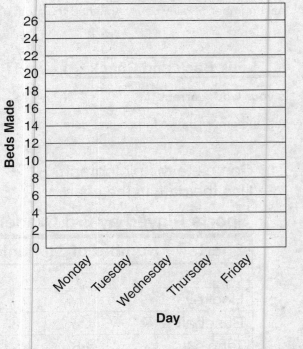

Number of Students
Who Made Beds

Problem-Solving Applications

Students' Favorite Dogs

Dog	Number Counted
Beagle	🐕 🐕 🐕
Collie	🐕 🐕 🐕 🐕 🐕
Shepherd	🐕 🐕 🐕
Poodle	🐕
Dalmation	🐕 🐕

Each 🐕 = 2 votes.

Students were asked to tell their favorite kind of dog. This pictograph shows how many students chose each kind of dog as their favorite. Use the pictograph to answer each exercise.

How many students chose a beagle? 6 students

Which dog had 5 votes? Shepherd

The chart below shows how many points a football team scored in each of a game's four quarters.

Quarter	Points Scored
1st	7
2nd	3
3rd	10
4th	6

1. Complete the bar graph.

2. How many points were scored in the 3rd quarter? _____

3. How many points were scored in the entire game? _____

Name_____

Car Wash

The third-grade class at Hawthorne Elementary School raised money to buy a new computer by having a car wash on the first Saturday of June.

Suppose the car wash began at 9:00 A.M. and ended at 1:00 P.M.

1. How many hours passed from the start to the finish of the car wash?   _____

2. The students took a break at 11:15 A.M. How much time passed from the start of the car wash until the break?

_____

The table shows how many cars were washed during each hour.

3. Use the table data to complete the bar graph for the number of cars washed each hour. The data for Hour 1 and Hour 3 are already completed.

Third-Grade Car Wash

Hour	Number of Cars
1	11
2	9
3	16
4	12

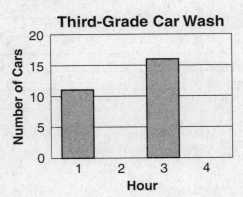

4. On which date in June did the car wash take place?

_____

June						
S	M	T	W	T	F	S
		1	2	3	4	5
6	7	8	9	10	11	12
13	14	15	16	17	18	19
20	21	22	23	24	25	26
27	28	29	30			

Name_____

Multiplication as Repeated Addition   R 5-1

Each of the groups below has the same number of squares.
There are 5 groups of 4. There are a total of 20 squares.

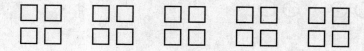

Here is the addition sentence for this problem: $4 + 4 + 4 + 4 + 4 = 20$

Here is the multiplication sentence for this problem: $5 \times 4 = 20$

Complete the addition and multiplication sentences.

1. ○○ ○○ ○○ ○○
   ○○ ○○ ○○ ○○

   4 groups of _____ $4 + 4 + 4 + 4 =$ _____ $4 \times$ _____ $= 16$

2. ○○○○   ○○○○   ○○○○   ○○○○
   ○○○   ○○○   ○○○   ○○○

   _____ groups of 7   _____ + _____ + _____ + _____ $= 28$

   $7 \times$ _____ $=$ _____

Write each addition sentence as a multiplication sentence.

3. $1 + 1 + 1 + 1 + 1 = 5$ _____

4. $8 + 8 + 8 = 24$ _____

Write each multiplication sentence as an addition sentence.

5. $5 \times 5 = 25$ _____

6. $6 \times 2 = 12$ _____

7. **Writing in Math** Juan says, "When you put together
   unequal groups, you can only add." Is he correct? Explain.

   _____

Multiplication as Repeated Addition   **P 5-1**

Complete each number sentence.

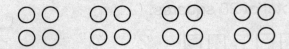

1. 4 groups of _____

2. _____ + _____ + _____ + _____ = 16

3. 4 × _____ = _____

4. Write an addition sentence and a multiplication sentence to show the total number of bicycle tires.

_____

_____

5. **Number Sense** Marlon has 4 baseball cards, Jake has 4 baseball cards, and Sam has 3 baseball cards. Can you write a multiplication sentence to find how many baseball cards they have altogether? Explain.

_____

_____

Test Prep

6. Which lets you put equal groups together?

   A. Division   **B.** Subtraction   **C.** Estimation   **D.** Multiplication

7. **Writing in Math** Explain what the product of a multiplication sentence is.

_____

_____

Arrays and Multiplication

An array shows objects in equal rows. This array shows 3 rows of 6 pennies.

The addition sentence for this array is
6 + 6 + 6 = 18.

The multiplication sentence for this array is
3 × 6 = 18.

Because of the Commutative (Order) Property of Multiplication, you can multiply the two numbers in any order:
3 × 6 = 18 and 6 × 3 = 18.

Write a multiplication sentence for each array.

1. ○○○○○○○
○○○○○○○   _____

2. ☐☐☐☐
☐☐☐☐
☐☐☐☐
☐☐☐☐   _____

Complete each multiplication sentence. You may use counters or draw a picture to help.

3. 3 × 4 = 12   _____ × 3 = 12   **4.** 5 × 2 = 10   2 × _____ = 10

5. Number Sense How can you use the commutative property to know that

○○○○○○
○○○○○○ is equal to
○○○○○○

○○○
○○○
○○○
○○○
○○○
○○○ ?

_____

_____

_____

Arrays and Multiplication

Draw an array to show each multiplication fact. Write the product.

1. $3 \times 6 =$ _____

2. $8 \times 3 =$ _____

Write a multiplication sentence for each array.

3. ○○○○○
   ○○○○○
   ○○○○○

   _____

4. ○○○○○○○○○
   ○○○○○○○○○

   _____

5. ○○○○○○
   ○○○○○○

   _____

Complete. You may use counters or draw a picture to help.

6. $3 \times 7 = 21$

   $7 \times$ _____ $= 21$

7. $2 \times$ _____ $= 18$

   $9 \times$ _____ $= 18$

8. $4 \times 5 =$ _____

   $5 \times 4 =$ _____

9. **Number Sense** Samantha says $1 + 1 + 1 = 3$ cannot be written as a multiplication sentence because there are no equal groups. Do you agree? Explain.

   _____

   _____

Test Prep

10. Which of the following is equal to 7×4?

    A. $7 - 4$ **B.** 4×7 **C.** $4 + 7$ **D.** $7 + 4$

11. **Writing in Math** Explain how you would build arrays for both of the multiplication sentences in the above exercise.

    _____

    _____

Name_____

Writing Multiplication Stories

When you write a multiplication story you should:

- Always end the story with a question.
- Draw a picture to show the main idea.

Example:

Write a multiplication story for 5 × 9.

Josephine has 5 friends over for a snack. She gives each friend 9 grapes. How many grapes did Josephine give altogether?

Josephine gave 45 grapes altogether.

Write a multiplication story for each exercise. Draw a picture to find each product.

1. 4 × 3

_____

_____

2. 5 × 2

_____

_____

3. 1 × 6

_____

_____

4. Number Sense Leshon mowed 7 lawns in his neighborhood. He made $5 for each lawn he mowed. Write a multiplication sentence to show how much money Leshon earned.

_____

© Pearson Education, Inc. 3

Writing Multiplication Stories

Write a multiplication story for each. Draw a picture to
find each product.

1. 8×4

_____

_____

2. 9×3

_____

_____

3. Patrick works at the frozen-yogurt store after school.
   Yesterday he sold 4 double-scoop strawberry cones. How
   many scoops of strawberry frozen yogurt did he use?

   _____

4. Fiona has 3 pet rabbits. Each rabbit eats 3 carrots a day. How
   many carrots does Fiona need each day to feed her rabbits?

   _____

5. **Algebra** Sara has pet spiders. She keeps all of the spiders in
   the same tank. There are 24 spider legs in the tank. How many
   spiders does Sara have in the tank? (Hint: a spider has 8 legs.)

   _____

Test Prep

6. How many factors are in the multiplication sentence $9 \times 4 = 36$?

   A. 1   **B.** 2   **C.** 3   **D.** 4

7. **Writing in Math** Write a multiplication story with the factors 2 and 5.

   _____

   _____

Name_____

PROBLEM-SOLVING STRATEGY
Make a Table

R 5-4

Planting For every flower Tonya plants, she will need to water it with 2 gal of water. How many gallons of water will she need for 6 plants?

Read and Understand

Step 1: What do you know?
You know how much water is needed for each plant.

Step 2: What are you trying to find?
You are trying to find how many gallons of water are needed for 6 plants.

Plan and Solve

What strategy will you use?
Strategy: Make a table.

First, set up your table with labels.

Number of flowers						
Gallons of water						

Enter the information you know.

Number of flowers	1	2	3			
Gallons of water	2	4	6			

Look for a pattern. Continue the table.

Find the answer in the table.

Number of flowers	1	2	3	4	5	6
Gallons of water	2	4	6	8	10	12

Tonya will need 12 gal of water to plant 6 flowers.

Complete the table to solve the problem. Write the answer in a complete sentence.

1. Mrs. Dolan's nursery school class uses crayons during coloring time. Each student gets 6 crayons. If there are 6 students, how many crayons are needed?

Number of students	1	2	3	4	5	6
Number of crayons	6	12				

© Pearson Education, Inc. 3

Name_____

Make a Table

Complete the table to solve the problem. Write the answer in a complete sentence.

1. Each centerpiece for the community banquet has 4 flowers in a vase. There needs to be 7 centerpieces. How many flowers will be used to fill the vases?

Number of vases	1	2	3	4	5	6	7
Number of flowers	4	8	12				

_____

2. Mrs. King bought 18 grapefruit at the market. Her family eats 3 grapefruit each day. How many days will the grapefruit last?

Number of grapefruit	18	15	12			
Number of days	1	2	3			

_____

3. Edmond saves $5 each week. How much will he have in his savings account at the end of 5 weeks?

Number of weeks	1	2					
Money saved	$5	$10					

_____

_____

4. **Reasoning** Will Edmond be able to buy a $36 skateboard at the end of 7 weeks? Explain.

_____

_____

Name_____

Multiple-Step Problems

Food Court Food court tickets cost $2 each. Susan bought a dinner and a dessert. How much did Susan spend?

Food Court Prices

Dinner	3 tickets
Dessert	2 tickets

Read and Understand

Find the hidden question.

How many tickets did Susan use?

$3 + 2 = 5$
Susan used 5 tickets at the food court.

Plan and Solve

Solve the problem.

How much did Susan spend?

$5 \text{ tickets} \times \$2 = \$10$
Susan spent $10 at the food court.

Write and answer the hidden question or questions. Then solve the problem. For 1–2, use the Balloon Prices list.

Balloon Prices

Small	Medium	Large
$1.00	$2.00	$3.00

1. Virginia wants 3 large balloons. How much money will she need?

   _____

   _____

   _____

2. Reese buys 2 medium balloons and 2 small balloons. He pays with a $10 bill. How much change will Reese get?

   _____

   _____

   _____

   _____

Name_____

PROBLEM-SOLVING SKILL
Multiple-Step Problems

Write and answer the hidden question or questions. Then solve the problem.

1. Dave swam 6 laps and did 9 dives at the swimming pool. Crystal did 4 dives and swam 8 laps. How many more laps than dives did Crystal and Dave do?

_____

_____

For 2–5, use the cookbook.

2. Polly has 8 strawberries, 1 c milk, and 10 ice cubes. She makes a strawberry smoothie. What ingredients does she have left?

_____

_____

Strawberry Smoothie	Banana Smoothie
6 strawberries	2 bananas
1 c milk	2 c milk
6 ice cubes	10 ice cubes
Blend on high speed 2 min	Blend on high speed 3 min
Serves 1	Serves 2

3. Matt wants to make both recipes. He has 2 dozen ice cubes. Does he have enough ice cubes? Explain.

_____

_____

4. Julian wants to make banana smoothies for himself and 3 of his friends. How many bananas will he need?

_____

_____

5. **Writing in Math** Use the smoothie recipes to write a word problem with a hidden question. Then solve the problem.

_____

_____

9 as a Factor

Patterns can help you remember multiplication facts with 9 as a factor.

9s Facts
$9 \times 0 = 0$
$9 \times 1 = 9$
$9 \times 2 = 18$
$9 \times 3 = 27$
$9 \times 4 = 36$
$9 \times 5 = 45$
$9 \times 6 = 54$
$9 \times 7 = 63$
$9 \times 8 = 72$
$9 \times 9 = 81$

Here is one pattern: The tens digit is always 1 less than the factor multiplied by 9.

For example:
$9 \times 6 = 54$. The factor 6 is multiplied by 9. One less than 6 is 5. The tens digit is 5.

Here is another pattern: The sum of the digits of the product always add to 9.

For example:
$9 \times 5 = 45$ $9 \times 3 = 27$
$4 + 5 = 9$ $2 + 7 = 9$

Find 9×7.

Use the patterns to help you find the answer.

$7 - 1 = 6$. The tens digit will be 6.
$9 - 6 = 3$. The ones digit will be 3.
$9 \times 7 = 63$

---

1. $9 \times 3 =$ _____

2. $2 \times 9 =$ _____

3. $\$9 \times 2 =$ _____

4. $4 \times 2 =$ _____

5. $9 \times 10 =$ _____

6. $6 \times 5 =$ _____

7. $9 \times 8 =$ _____

8. $\$2 \times 2 =$ _____

9. $6 \times \$9 =$ _____

10.
$$\begin{array}{r} \$9 \\ \times\ 9 \\ \hline \end{array}$$

11.
$$\begin{array}{r} 10 \\ \times\ 6 \\ \hline \end{array}$$

12.
$$\begin{array}{r} 9 \\ \times\ 0 \\ \hline \end{array}$$

13. Multiply 9 and 7. _____

14. **Writing in Math** Look at the table of 9s facts. Can you think of another number pattern in the multiples of 9? Explain.

_____

_____

9 as a Factor

1. $9 \times 4 = $ _____   **2.** $7 \times 9 = $ _____   **3.** $\$9 \times 9 = $ _____

4. $0 \times 9 = $ _____   **5.** $9 \times 3 = $ _____   **6.** $9 \times 2 = $ _____

7. $\begin{array}{r} 9 \\ \times\ 5 \\ \hline \end{array}$ **8.** $\begin{array}{r} 10 \\ \times\ 9 \\ \hline \end{array}$ **9.** $\begin{array}{r} \$2 \\ \times\ 9 \\ \hline \end{array}$ **10.** $\begin{array}{r} 9 \\ \times\ 6 \\ \hline \end{array}$ **11.** $\begin{array}{r} 9 \\ \times\ 1 \\ \hline \end{array}$

12. Multiply 4 and 9. _____   **13.** Find 3 times 9. _____

14. Paula's mother put Paula's hair into 9 braids. Each braid used 3 beads. How many beads did Paula's mother use?

_____

15. Number the fingers to help multiply 5×9. Cross out the finger you could bend down to show 5×9. Find 5×9.

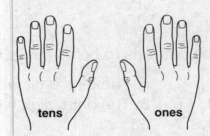

tens   ones

_____

16. **Number Sense** Explain how the finger pattern helped you find 5×9.

_____

_____

_____

Test Prep

17. $2 + 2 + 2 + 2 + 2 + 2 + 2 + 2 + 2 = $ _____

A. 2×9 **B.** $2 + 9$ **C.** 9×9 **D.** $9 - 2$

18. **Writing in Math** Write a multiplication story for 9×8.

_____

_____

Practicing Multiplication Facts

Here is how to make a set of flashcards.

- Write the first part of a multiplication fact on the front of the card.
- Write the product on the back.

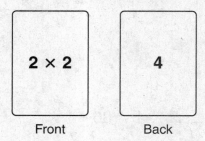

Front   Back

Invite a partner to make a set of 10 flashcards while you also make 10 flashcards. Use them to play a game together. Hold a flashcard so that the multiplication fact (the front) faces your partner and the product (the back) faces you. Have your partner say the product without looking at the back of the flashcard. Take turns holding the flashcards for each other.

1. $4 \times 9 = $ _____   **2.** $2 \times 6 = $ _____   **3.** $5 \times 4 = $ _____

4. $10 \times 2 = $ _____   **5.** $6 \times 1 = $ _____   **6.** $2 \times 7 = $ _____

7. $9 \times 8 = $ _____   **8.** $7 \times 1 = $ _____   **9.** $6 \times 1 = $ _____

10. $2 \times 7 = $ _____   **11.** $9 \times 8 = $ _____   **12.** $7 \times 1 = $ _____

13. $\begin{array}{r} 9 \\ \times\ 7 \\ \hline \end{array}$ **14.** $\begin{array}{r} 5 \\ \times\ 5 \\ \hline \end{array}$ **15.** $\begin{array}{r} 9 \\ \times\ 3 \\ \hline \end{array}$ **16.** $\begin{array}{r} 5 \\ \times\ 2 \\ \hline \end{array}$

17. **Number Sense** Shawna thinks that $8 \times 2 = 17$. What number pattern shows that she is not correct?

_____

Algebra Write the missing number.

18. $10 \times $ _____ $ = 50$ **19.** $9 \times $ _____ $ = 36$ **20.** _____ $ \times 5 = 45$

Name_____

Practicing Multiplication Facts

1. $9 \times 8 = $ _____   **2.** $5 \times 4 = $ _____   **3.** $1 \times 2 = $ _____

4. $7 \times 0 = $ _____   **5.** $8 \times 10 = $ _____   **6.** $6 \times 2 = $ _____

7.   5   **8.**   3   **9.**   9   **10.**   1   **11.**   2
$\underline{\times\ 6}$ $\underline{\times\ 5}$ $\underline{\times\ 4}$ $\underline{\times\ 1}$ $\underline{\times\ 7}$

Algebra Write the missing numbers.

12. $7 \times$ _____ $= 0$ **13.** _____ $\times 4 = 36$

14. $2 \times$ _____ $= 4$ **15.** $8 \times$ _____ $= 40$

16. Number Sense Is 30 a multiple of 5? How do you know?

_____

_____

17. Seven friends went to the carnival. Each spent $0.20
on tickets. How much did they spend altogether on
the tickets?   _____

Test Prep

18. Which is the product of 1×0?

   A. 9×9 **B.** 0×9 **C.** 9×1 **D.** 1×9

19. Writing in Math Stacy multiplied 5×9 and said the
answer was 44. What two patterns could you use to show
that her answer is not correct?

_____

_____

_____

_____

Name_____

Dozens of Eggs!

At United States chicken farms, female chickens lay about 5 eggs per week. How many eggs would the chicken lay after 6 weeks?

You can make a table to solve this problem.

First, draw your table and enter the information you know.

Week	1	2	3	4	5	6
Eggs laid	5					

Then look for a pattern and continue the table.

Week	1	2	3	4	5	6
Eggs laid	5	10	15	20	25	30

After 6 weeks, the chicken will have laid about 30 eggs.

1. Tim collects eggs each morning on his family farm. If he collects 7 eggs each morning, how many eggs will he have after 7 days? Complete the table to solve this problem.

Day	1	2	3	4	5	6	7
Eggs collected	7						

2. Suppose there are 2 eggs in a carton. How many eggs will you have if you buy 3 cartons? 7 cartons? 9 cartons?

_____

3. Suppose there are 5 eggs in a carton. How many eggs will you have if you buy 4 cartons? 8 cartons? 10 cartons?

_____

4. Suppose there are 9 eggs in a carton. How many eggs will you have if you buy 5 cartons? 7 cartons? 9 cartons?

_____

Name_____

Measure Your Lunch

Liquid and dry measurements use either customary units or metric units. If you go to a supermarket today or simply look in the kitchen, you will see that many of the products your family buys have both customary units and metric unit information.

1. A small can of soup weighs about 10 oz. Write an addition sentence and a multiplication sentence for about how many ounces of soup there are in 7 cans.

   _____

   _____

2. One serving of chicken-with-rice soup contains 8 g of carbohydrates. How many grams of carbohydrates are there in 5 servings of the soup?   _____

3. One can of condensed chicken-with-rice soup contains 5 g of protein. Finish the table to find the total amount of protein in different numbers of cans.

Number of cans	1	2									
Grams of protein	5	10									

4. A small container of mixed-berry yogurt has 10 mg of cholesterol. How many milligrams of cholesterol are there in 4 small containers of mixed-berry yogurt?

   _____

5. A small container of mixed-berry yogurt also has 9 g of protein. The recommended daily allowance of protein is about 45 grams. About how many small containers of mixed-berry yogurt do you have to eat to get the recommended daily amount of protein?

   _____

3 as a Factor

You can use an array to show multiplication. The number of rows is the first factor, and the number of columns is the second factor.

What You Show	**What You Think**
(1) (3)	$3 \times 1 = 3$
(2) (2)	$2 \times 2 = 4$

Complete the arrays.

$3 \times 5 = $ _____

○○○○○
○○○○○

$2 \times$ _____ $= $ _____

○○○○○

$1 \times$ _____ $= $ _____

$3 \times$ _____ $= 15$

---

1. $3 \times 2 = $ _____

2. $3 \times 4 = $ _____

3. $3 \times 5 = $ _____

4. $\begin{array}{r} 3 \\ \times\ 8 \\ \hline \end{array}$

5. $\begin{array}{r} 3 \\ \times\ 9 \\ \hline \end{array}$

6. $\begin{array}{r} 7 \\ \times\ 3 \\ \hline \end{array}$

7. Number Sense Each of 3 dogs has 6 puppies. How many puppies are there altogether?

_____

Name_____

3 as a Factor

1. $1 \times 3 =$ _____   **2.** $3 \times 7 =$ _____   **3.** $\$6 \times 3 =$ _____

4. $8 \times 3 =$ _____   **5.** $3 \times 8 =$ _____   **6.** $3 \times 5 =$ _____

7. $\begin{array}{r} 3 \\ \times\ 2 \\ \hline \end{array}$ **8.** $\begin{array}{r} 4 \\ \times\ 3 \\ \hline \end{array}$ **9.** $\begin{array}{r} 3 \\ \times\ 0 \\ \hline \end{array}$ **10.** $\begin{array}{r} \$3 \\ \times\ 5 \\ \hline \end{array}$ **11.** $\begin{array}{r} 3 \\ \times\ 9 \\ \hline \end{array}$

12. Number Sense What two multiplication facts can be added to find 3×7?

_____

13. There were 5 people who bought tickets to a football game. They each bought 3 tickets. How many tickets were bought altogether?   _____

14. Marina has 3 colors of flowers. She has 3 of each color. How many flowers does she have altogether?   _____

15. A group of 7 friends paid $3 each to get into a carnival. How much did they pay altogether?   _____

Test Prep

16. Tom gave each of his 5 friends 3 stickers. How many stickers did he give away?

A. 3 stickers   **B.** 5 stickers   **C.** 12 stickers   **D.** 15 stickers

17. Writing in Math Explain how you can break apart 3×9 to help you multiply.

_____

_____

_____

4 as a Factor

If you know a 2s multiplication fact, you can find a 4s multiplication fact.

When you double an array of 2 × 1, you get an array of 4 × 1.

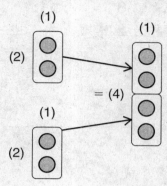

This shows that if you double a 2s fact, or add the 2s fact to itself, you can find the 4s fact.

$(2 \times 1) + (2 \times 1) = (4 \times 1)$
$2 + 2 = 4$

---

1. 4 × 1 = _____

2. 4 × 2 = _____

3. 4 × 7 = _____

4. 4 × 3 = _____

5. 4
  × 9

6. 4
  × 6

7. 5
  × 4

8. 4
  × $8

9. Number Sense How can you use 2 × 10 to find 4 × 10?

_____

_____

_____

_____

Name_____

4 as a Factor

1. $2 \times 4 =$ _____   2. $4 \times 5 =$ _____   3. $3 \times 4 =$ _____

4. $4 \times 4 =$ _____   5. $\$4 \times 8 =$ _____   6. $4 \times 6 =$ _____

7. $\begin{array}{r} 1 \\ \times\ 4 \\ \hline \end{array}$ 8. $\begin{array}{r} 4 \\ \times\ 4 \\ \hline \end{array}$ 9. $\begin{array}{r} \$4 \\ \times\ 9 \\ \hline \end{array}$ 10. $\begin{array}{r} 0 \\ \times\ 4 \\ \hline \end{array}$ 11. $\begin{array}{r} 4 \\ \times\ 7 \\ \hline \end{array}$

12. **Number Sense** What multiplication fact can you double to find 4×7?

    _____

13. Continue each pattern.

    a. 20, 16, 12, _____, _____, _____

    b. 20, 24, 28, _____, _____, _____

    c. 8, 12, 16, _____, _____, _____

14. There are 6 chairs around a table. Each chair has 4 legs. How many chair legs are around the table?

    _____

15. Sally bought 4 movie tickets for herself and her friends. The tickets cost $8 each. How much money did Sally spend on the movie tickets?

    _____

Test Prep

16. Aaron changed the tires on 5 cars. Each car had 4 tires. How many tires did Aaron change?

    A. 12 tires   **B.** 16 tires   **C.** 20 tires   **D.** 24 tires

17. **Writing in Math** Tessie multiplied 3×4, and then doubled it to find 6×8. Did she get the correct answer? Explain.

    _____

    _____

6 and 7 as Factors

You can use multiplication facts that you already know to find multiplication facts you are unsure of.
You know the multiplication facts for 1s, 2s, and 5s.

Find 9×6.

Break apart an array for 9×6 into two separate arrays. Make one array for 5×6 in order to use your knowledge of 5s facts. Make the second array 4×6.

$5 \times 6 = 30$

$4 \times 6 = 24$

$30 + 24 = 54$, so $9 \times 6 = 54$

Find 7×8.

You can do the same thing to multiply by 7.
Break the array for 7×8 into two separate arrays:
one for 5×8 and one for 2×8.

$5 \times 8 = 40$

$2 \times 8 = 16$

$40 + 16 = 56$, so $7 \times 8 = 56$

1. $2 \times 7 =$ _____   2. $5 \times 7 =$ _____   3. $7 \times 9 =$ _____

4. $6 \times 4 =$ _____   5. $6 \times 6 =$ _____   6. $6 \times \$10 =$ _____

7.   4   8.   8   9.   \$7   10.   5
  $\times\ 7$ $\times\ 6$ $\times\ 3$ $\times\ 9$

11. **Number Sense** Harold says "To find 6×8, I can use the facts for 5×4 and 1×4." Do you agree? Explain.

_____

_____

Name_____

6 and 7 as Factors

1. $5 \times 6 =$ _____   2. $6 \times 3 =$ _____   3. $6 \times 8 =$ _____

4. $\$3 \times 7 =$ _____   5. $7 \times 10 =$ _____   6. $7 \times 4 =$ _____

7. $\$4$ 8.   5   9.   7   10.   6   11.   6
   $\times\ 6$ $\times\ 7$ $\times\ 8$ $\times\ 6$ $\times\ 7$

12. Multiply 7 and 7. _____   13. Multiply 1 and 6. _____

14. Find the product
    of 6 and 9. _____   15. Find 7 times 2. _____

16. **Number Sense** What multiplication fact can be
    found by using the arrays for 2×9 and 5×9?   _____

17. Raul's science class is hatching chicken eggs.
    If the eggs take 3 weeks to hatch, how many
    days until they hatch?   _____

18. Emily cut 7 apples into slices. There are 6 slices
    from each apple. How many apple slices did
    she cut in all?   _____

Test Prep

19. Helen needs 6 more stuffed miniature bears to complete
    her collection. Each bear costs $9. How much will Helen
    have to spend to complete her collection?

    A. $45   **B.** $54   **C.** $56   **D.** $63

20. **Writing in Math** Explain how you could use $5 \times 6 = 30$ to
    find the product of 6×6.

    _____

    _____

    _____

8 as a Factor

You can use doubling to help multiply with 8.

Find 8×6.

You can double a 4s fact to multiply with 8.

First, find $4 \times 6 = 24$.

Then double the product.

○ ○ ○ ○ ○ ○
○ ○ ○ ○ ○ ○ $4 \times 6 = 24$
○ ○ ○ ○ ○ ○
○ ○ ○ ○ ○ ○

$24 + 24 = 48$

○ ○ ○ ○ ○ ○
○ ○ ○ ○ ○ ○ $4 \times 6 = 24$
○ ○ ○ ○ ○ ○
○ ○ ○ ○ ○ ○

So, $8 \times 6 = 48$.

Find 8×8.

$$4 \times 8 = 32$$
$$\underline{4 \times 8 = 32}$$
$$8 \times 8 = 64$$

---

1. $2 \times 8 = $ _____

2. $4 \times 8 = $ _____

3. $8 \times 5 = $ _____

4. $5 \times 6 = $ _____

5. $\begin{array}{r} 0 \\ \times\ 8 \\ \hline \end{array}$

6. $\begin{array}{r} 8 \\ \times\ 3 \\ \hline \end{array}$

7. $\begin{array}{r} 9 \\ \times\ 8 \\ \hline \end{array}$

8. $\begin{array}{r} 8 \\ \times\ 10 \\ \hline \end{array}$

9. Number Sense Name a multiplication fact that can help you with 8×4, and tell how.

_____

_____

Name_____

8 as a Factor

1. $1 \times 8 =$ _____   **2.** $8 \times 0 =$ _____   **3.** $\$8 \times 3 =$ _____

4. $2 \times 8 =$ _____   **5.** $8 \times 7 =$ _____   **6.** $8 \times 6 =$ _____

7. $\begin{array}{r} \$3 \\ \times\ 8 \\ \hline \end{array}$ **8.** $\begin{array}{r} 8 \\ \times\ 1 \\ \hline \end{array}$ **9.** $\begin{array}{r} 4 \\ \times\ 8 \\ \hline \end{array}$ **10.** $\begin{array}{r} 8 \\ \times\ 9 \\ \hline \end{array}$ **11.** $\begin{array}{r} 8 \\ \times\ 5 \\ \hline \end{array}$

12. An octopus has 8 arms. At the zoo, there were
3 octopuses in one tank. How many arms were
in the tank altogether?   _____

13. For every hour Carrie works at the restaurant,
she earns $8. She worked 7 hr yesterday.
How much did she earn?   _____

Test Prep

14. Each package of cheese contains 10 slices. Each package
of rolls contains 8 rolls. Ted bought 5 packages of each.
How many rolls did he buy?

A. 35 rolls   **B.** 40 rolls   **C.** 50 rolls   **D.** 80 rolls

15. **Writing in Math** Carlos used two arrays
to find 8×6. Fix Carlos's error and then
give the correct answer.   _____

$\begin{array}{ccc} \bigcirc & \bigcirc & \bigcirc \\ \bigcirc & \bigcirc & \bigcirc \\ \bigcirc & \bigcirc & \bigcirc \\ \bigcirc & \bigcirc & \bigcirc \end{array}$ $\begin{array}{ccc} \bigcirc & \bigcirc & \bigcirc \\ \bigcirc & \bigcirc & \bigcirc \\ \bigcirc & \bigcirc & \bigcirc \\ \bigcirc & \bigcirc & \bigcirc \end{array}$

74 Use with Lesson 6-4.

Practicing Multiplication Facts

You can use more than one strategy to find the same multiplication fact.

Find 6×4.

You can switch the order of the factors in a multiplication problem and still have the same result. 6×4 is the same as 4×6. If you know the fact that $4 \times 6 = 24$, then you also know the fact that $6 \times 4 = 24$. This is called the Commutative Property of Addition.

Some facts can be added to find facts that you do not know. You can combine 5×4 and 1×4 to find 6×4. $5 \times 4 = 20$ and $1 \times 4 = 4$. $20 + 4 = 24$, so $6 \times 4 = 24$.

Some facts can be doubled to find facts that you do not know.
2s facts can be doubled to find 4s facts.
4s facts can be doubled to find 8s facts.

6×4 is the same as 4×6. Double the 2s fact for 6. $6 \times 2 = 12$. 12 doubled is 24. $6 \times 4 = 24$.

---

1. $2 \times 9 = $ _____

2. $5 \times 7 = $ _____

3. $5 \times 8 = $ _____

4. $7 \times 8 = $ _____

5.
$$\begin{array}{r} 6 \\ \times\ 5 \\ \hline \end{array}$$

6.
$$\begin{array}{r} 4 \\ \times\ 9 \\ \hline \end{array}$$

7.
$$\begin{array}{r} 5 \\ \times\ 9 \\ \hline \end{array}$$

8.
$$\begin{array}{r} 8 \\ \times\ 6 \\ \hline \end{array}$$

9. Number Sense Darien does not know the fact for 6×5. Tell two ways that will help him find the product without adding together five 6s.

_____

_____

_____

_____

Name_____

Practicing Multiplication Facts

1. $8 \times 3 =$ _____   **2.** $4 \times 7 =$ _____   **3.** $6 \times 8 =$ _____

4. $5 \times 9 =$ _____   **5.** $7 \times 8 =$ _____   **6.** $5 \times 7 =$ _____

7. $\begin{array}{r} 6 \\ \times\ 2 \\ \hline \end{array}$ **8.** $\begin{array}{r} 4 \\ \times\ 6 \\ \hline \end{array}$ **9.** $\begin{array}{r} 10 \\ \times\ 0 \\ \hline \end{array}$ **10.** $\begin{array}{r} 3 \\ \times\ 5 \\ \hline \end{array}$ **11.** $\begin{array}{r} 4 \\ \times\ 9 \\ \hline \end{array}$

12. **Number Sense** How can you use the multiplication facts for 3 to help you find the multiplication facts for 9?

_____

_____

13. Lee puts 4 napkins on each tray. Complete the table.

Trays	1	2	3	4	5
Napkins	4				

14. How many napkins will Lee have on 10 trays? _____

Test Prep

15. Linda gets $6 for each dog that she walks. Yesterday she walked 5 dogs, and today she walked 2 dogs. How much did Linda make in two days for walking the dogs?

A. $12   **B.** $30   **C.** $42   **D.** $48

16. **Writing in Math** Explain another way to help you find the product of 8×6 without using repeated addition.

_____

_____

_____

Name_____

Look for a Pattern

Dots Pattern Here is a pattern with dots. What will the 5th and
6th pictures look like?

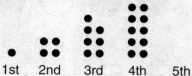

1st   2nd   3rd   4th   5th   6th

Read and Understand

Step 1: What do you know?

The number of dots in the first four pictures.

Step 2: What are you trying to find?

The number of dots for the 5th and 6th pictures.

Plan and Solve

Step 3: What strategy will you use?

Strategy: Look for a pattern.

There are 3 more dots in the 2nd picture than in the 1st picture.

There are 3 more dots in the 3rd picture than in the 2nd picture.

The number of dots increases by 3 each time.

Answer: There will be 13 dots in the 5th picture and 16 dots in the 6th picture.

Look Back and Check

Step 4: Is your work correct?
Yes, the "increases by 3" pattern works for all of the pictures.

Complete the pattern. Then tell what the pattern is.

1. ○ □ △ △ ○ ___ ___

_____

_____

2. What are the missing numbers in the pattern below?

3, 8, 13, _____, _____, 28, _____

_____

Name_____

Look for a Pattern

Describe patterns you see. Write the answer in a complete sentence.

1. Dillon is making a necklace with black and white beads. Which colors will be used for the next 3 beads?

_____

_____

_____

2. Nancy is making a pattern using circles. How many circles will she draw for the next design in the pattern?

_____

_____

_____

_____

3. Alisha was walking on a sidewalk and noticed the pattern below in the color of the blocks. She walked over 27 blocks that were in the pattern. How many darker blocks did she walk over?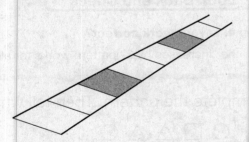

_____

4. **Writing in Math** Linda has 18 quarters, 12 dimes, and 7 pennies. She wants to make a pattern of quarter, quarter, penny, dime, and quarter. How many of these patterns can she make? Explain.

_____

_____

Using Multiplication to Compare

The word *times* in a word problem means multiplication. If you have 3 times as many pencils as Joe does, it means that however many pencils Joe has, you have his pencils multiplied by 3.

Pencil	Pencil					—→ Number of pencils

Pencil	Pencil	Pencil	Pencil	Pencil	Pencil	—→ 3 times as many pencils

The words *twice as many* or *2 times as many* mean to multiply by 2.

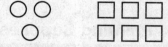

There are twice as many squares as there are circles.

1. Sara has twice as many ribbons as Harriet. Harriet has 6 ribbons. How many ribbons does Sarah have?

   _____

6		—→ Harriet's ribbons

6	6	—→ Sara's ribbons

2. Luke is 6 years old. Danny is 3 times his age. How old is Danny?

   _____

3. Paula has 3 rings. Kenya has 4 times as many rings. How many rings does Kenya have?

   _____

4. **Number Sense** If Leroy has 9 sports cards, and Steve has 3 times as many, how many sports cards does Steve have?

   _____

5. Jill invited 6 friends to her party. Mara invited twice as many to her sleepover. How many friends were invited to Mara's sleepover?

   _____

Name_____

Using Multiplication to Compare

1. Jim has lost 3 times as many teeth as his brother Justin. Justin has lost 3 teeth. How many teeth has Jim lost?

Teeth Justin Lost	3
Teeth Jim Lost	

_____

2. Sarah has 6 seashells. She has 7 times as many pieces of beach glass as she does seashells. How many pieces of beach glass does she have? _____

3. The hardware store stocks 3 times as many gallons of white paint as they do gallons of gray paint. How many gallons of white paint are kept in stock at the hardware store?

Painting Supplies

Item	Number
Large paintbrush	12
Small paintbrush	18
Black paint	3
Gray paint	6
Green paint	4
Red paint	6
White paint	

_____

4. Number Sense Tom has $8. Becky has 4 times as many dollars as Tom. How much money do they have altogether?

_____

Test Prep

5. Gina's house has 9 windows. Jonathan's house has twice as many windows as Gina's. How many windows are in Jonathan's house?

A. 9 windows   **B.** 18 windows   **C.** 21 windows   **D.** 27 windows

6. Writing in Math Katie picked 7 times as many strawberries as Garrett. Garrett picked 6 quarts of strawberries. How many quarts did Katie pick? Which two multiplication facts can you use to help find the solution?

_____

_____

Patterns on a Table

Use the fact table to find 9×5. Find the 9 across the top and count down 6 spaces. Then find the 5 along the side and count across 10 spaces. The box where the column and the row meet is the product. For 9×5, follow the 9s column down and the 5s row across. The box where they meet is 45, so $9 \times 5 = 45$.

×	0	1	2	3	4	5	6	7	8	9	10	11	12
0	0	0	0	0	0	0	0	0	0	0	0	0	0
1	0	1	2	3	4	5	6	7	8	9	10	11	12
2	0	2	4	6	8	10	12	14	16	18	20	22	24
3	0	3	6	9	12	15	18	21	24	27	30	33	36
4	0	4	8	12	16	20	24	28	32	36	40	44	48
5	0	5	10	15	20	25	30	35	40	45	50	55	60
6	0	6	12	18	24	30	36	42	48	54	60	66	72
7	0	7	14	21	28	35	42	49	56	63	70	77	84
8	0	8	16	24	32	40	48	56	64	72	80	88	96
9	0	9	18	27	36	45	54	63	72	81	90	99	108
10	0	10	20	30	40	50	60	70	80	90	100	110	120
11	0	11	22	33	44	55	66	77	88	99	110	121	132
12	0	12	24	36	48	60	72	84	96	108	120	132	144

1. $4 \times 7 =$ _____   **2.** $5 \times 3 =$ _____

3. $0 \times 4 =$ _____   **4.** $3 \times 6 =$ _____

5. $\begin{array}{r} 7 \\ \times\ 2 \\ \hline \end{array}$ **6.** $\begin{array}{r} 1 \\ \times\ 5 \\ \hline \end{array}$ **7.** $\begin{array}{r} 9 \\ \times\ 3 \\ \hline \end{array}$ **8.** $\begin{array}{r} 6 \\ \times\ 7 \\ \hline \end{array}$

9. Writing in Math Skye has 6 bags of balloons. Each bag contains 4 balloons. How many balloons does Skye have altogether? Explain how you can use the multiplication table to help find the answer.

_____

_____

Patterns on a Table

1. $3 \times 9 =$ _____
2. $11 \times 10 =$ _____
3. $5 \times 7 =$ _____

4. $8 \times 7 =$ _____
5. $12 \times 4 =$ _____
6. $11 \times 5 =$ _____

7. $\begin{array}{r} 12 \\ \times\ 6 \\ \hline \end{array}$
8. $\begin{array}{r} 11 \\ \times\ 12 \\ \hline \end{array}$
9. $\begin{array}{r} 9 \\ \times\ 7 \\ \hline \end{array}$
10. $\begin{array}{r} 3 \\ \times\ 8 \\ \hline \end{array}$
11. $\begin{array}{r} 12 \\ \times\ 4 \\ \hline \end{array}$

12. **Number Sense** Could there be a number in the 2s column on the multiplication table that ends in a 5? Explain why or why not.

_____

_____

_____

13. A mouse eats about 11 calories each day.
    About how many calories does it eat in 8 days? _____

Test Prep

14. George and Shelley filled egg cartons with decorated eggs. A dozen eggs fits into each carton. They filled 6 cartons. How many decorated eggs did they have?

    A. 54 eggs   **B.** 60 eggs   **C.** 66 eggs   **D.** 72 eggs

15. **Writing in Math** Explain how you could use a 10s fact to find a 9s fact.

_____

_____

_____

_____

© Pearson Education, Inc. 3

Multiplying with Three Factors

When more than two factors are being multiplied, you can multiply them in any order and the product will be the same. This is called the Associative (grouping) Property of Multiplication.

Here are three different ways to multiply $6 \times 5 \times 4$.

Multiply the 6 and 5 first.	Multiply the 5 and 4 first.	Multiply the 6 and 4 first.
$(6 \times 5) \times 4$	$6 \times (5 \times 4)$	$(6 \times 4) \times 5$
$30 \times 4 = 120$	$6 \times 20 = 120$	$24 \times 5 = 120$

In each example, the product is the same. This means that you can find the easiest way to multiply more than two numbers.

1. $3 \times 2 \times 1 =$ _____

2. $2 \times 3 \times 5 =$ _____

3. $3 \times 3 \times 2 =$ _____

4. $7 \times 2 \times 1 =$ _____

5. $4 \times 7 \times 2 =$ _____

6. $5 \times 1 \times 2 =$ _____

7. $5 \times 2 \times 4 =$ _____

8. $4 \times 0 \times 3 =$ _____

9. $1 \times 0 \times 4 =$ _____

10. $3 \times 4 \times 5 =$ _____

11. $1 \times 4 \times 6 =$ _____

12. $2 \times 2 \times 6 =$ _____

13. $4 \times 1 \times 7 =$ _____

14. $8 \times 2 \times 1 =$ _____

15. Number Sense How do you know that $4 \times 2 \times 2$ is the same as 4×4? Explain.

_____

_____

_____

Name_____

Multiplying with Three Factors

1. $1 \times 2 \times 3 = $ _____
2. $2 \times 2 \times 4 = $ _____
3. $8 \times 2 \times 2 = $ _____

4. $6 \times 2 \times 1 = $ _____
5. $5 \times 5 \times 2 = $ _____
6. $3 \times 3 \times 3 = $ _____

7. $1 \times 7 \times 8 = $ _____
8. $0 \times 9 \times 8 = $ _____
9. $6 \times 2 \times 5 = $ _____

10. Number Sense Harvey says $9 \times 8 \times$ (any other number) will always be greater than the product of $2 \times 9 \times 4$. Do you agree? Explain.

_____

_____

_____

11. Write three ways to find $3 \times 2 \times 4$.

_____

12. Sarah and Amanda each have 2 bags with 4 marbles in each. How many marbles do they have altogether?   _____

13. Jesse bought 2 sheets of stamps. On each sheet there are 5 rows of stamps with 6 stamps in each row. How many stamps did Jesse buy?   _____

Test Prep

14. Which is the product of $2 \times 3 \times 2$?

A. 6   **B.** 7   **C.** 10   **D.** 12

15. Writing in Math A classroom has 6 tables. The teacher puts 2 pencils, 1 eraser, and 1 sheet of stickers into each bag, and puts 4 bags on each table. How many pencils did the teacher put in the bags altogether? Write a multiplication sentence and solve the problem.

_____

Find a Rule

David is cooking pancakes. He makes 3 pancakes for each person in his family. Today he needs to make pancakes for 9 people. He isn't sure how many he needs to make. If David used a table, he would see a rule for a pattern between the number of pancakes and the number of people eating those pancakes.

Number of people	1	2	3
Number of pancakes	3	6	

The rule for the pattern is multiply by 3. To make pancakes for 9 people, he takes the number of people, 9, and follows the rule, multiply by 3, to find that he needs to make 27 pancakes.

Write a rule for each table. Complete the table.

1.

Number of tents	1	2	3	4	5
Number of hikers	4	8	12		

2.

In	3	4	1	2	7
Out	15	20	5		

3.

In	2	4	6	8	10
Out	14	28			

4. **Number Sense** Chris can sand 7 planks in 1 hour. How many planks can he sand in 3 hours?

_____

Name_____

Find a Rule

Write a rule for each table. Complete the table.

1.

Number of boxes	1	2	3	4	5
Number of grapefruits	4	8			

_____

2.

Number of people	1	2	3	4	5
Number of fingers	10	20			

_____

3.

In	6	2	7	1	4
Out	18	6	21		

4. **Number Sense** Caleb filled baskets with flowers. He filled 5 baskets with the same number of roses in each basket. He used 35 roses. How many roses went into each basket? _____

Test Prep

5. The rule for a table is *Multiply by 5.* If a 3 is the **In** number, what is the **Out** number?

   A. 15   **B.** 10   **C.** 5   **D.** 3

6. **Writing in Math** What is the multiplication rule for this table? Why doesn't the rule *Add 6* work? Complete the table.

In	6	7	8	9	10
Out	12				20

_____

_____

_____

PROBLEM-SOLVING SKILL

Choose an Operation

New Restaurant A new restaurant opened and hired 2 new people a day for the first 6 days. How many new people were hired?

Read and Understand

Show the main idea.

Day 1   Day 2   Day 3

Day 4   Day 5   Day 6

Plan and Solve

Choose an operation.

Multiply to find the total when you put together equal groups.

$6 \times 2 = 12$

So, 12 new people were hired.

Draw a picture to show the main idea. Choose an operation, and solve the problem.

1. Every student who earned more than $100 for his or her school in a fund drive was given 4 movie passes. There were 8 students at the school who earned over $100. How many movie passes were given out at the school?

Name_____

PROBLEM-SOLVING SKILL

Choose an Operation

Draw a picture to show the main idea. Then choose an operation and solve the problem.

Sam joined a movie club that gives 4 points for every DVD movie. Sam can use his points to get the items on the flyer.

1. Sam has bought 7 DVD movies so far. How many points has he earned?

2. Sam exchanges some of his points for the movie passes. How many points does he have left?

3. Sam wants the baseball cap. He can use the points he has left. How many more points does Sam need to get the cap? How many more DVD movies will he need to buy?

Name _____

Terms

The word *term* means how long a person will perform an elected duty. The chart below shows how long a term is for the president, senators, and representatives of the United States government.

Elected Position	Term
President	4 years
Senator	6 years
U.S. representative	2 years

A president can only serve 2 terms. How many years is that?

You would use multiplication to solve this problem. If 1 term equals 4 years, then 2 terms equal 8 years.

4 years		$\longrightarrow$ 1 term
4 years	4 years	$\longrightarrow$ $2 \times 4 = 8$ years

---

1. For how many years would a representative serve if he or she served 3 terms?

   _____

2. If a representative served 5 terms, how many years would it be?

   _____

3. In 1991, the state of Colorado passed a law stating that a U.S. representative from that state could serve a maximum of 6 terms. How many years equal 6 terms?

   _____

4. If a senator serves 7 terms, how many years would it be?

   _____

5. **Number Sense** Which is longer, 2 terms as senator or 7 terms as a representative? How do you know?

   _____

   _____

Name_____

Television

In 2002, there were 10 national and international stations. There were also 56 national cable-program channels. A newspaper lists the TV-programming schedule each day for evening viewing from 8:00 P.M. until 12:30 A.M.

1. During that time period, 8 cable stations will show 2 movies each. How many movies will be shown then?   _____

2. During that same period, 6 other cable stations will show 3 movies each. How many movies will be shown by those 6 cable stations?   _____

3. From 8:00 P.M. to 12:30 A.M., 6 of the network channels will each have a total of 5 programs. How many programs will be shown by those channels?   _____

4. There are 4 cable channels that will show nine 30-minute programs during this period. How many programs will be shown by those 4 cable channels?   _____

5. Between 8:00 P.M. and 12:30 A.M., Network A shows 7 programs, Network B shows 6 programs, Network C shows 5 programs, and Network D shows 9 programs. Which networks show more programs altogether, Networks A and B, or Networks C and D? Explain.

_____

_____

A newspaper costs $0.50 an issue. Suppose you bought the newspaper using only one type of coin, either dimes, nickels, or pennies.

6. How many dimes would you need to buy a newspaper?   _____

7. How many nickels would you need?   _____

8. How many pennies would you need?   _____

Name_____

Division as Sharing

You can use counters to show division problems:

There are 6 shirts and 3 boxes. How many shirts fit in each box?

First, use 6 counters
for the 6 shirts.

Since the problem is
6 divided by 3, divide
the counters into
3 equal groups.

There are 2 counters
in each group.
Since 6 ÷ 3 = 2, two shirts
can fit in each box.

Use counters or draw a picture to solve.

1. 12 markers   3 boxes

How many markers in each box?

_____

2. 10 pencils   2 pencil cases

How many pencils in each pencil case?

_____

3. 9 tadpoles   3 tanks

How many tadpoles in each tank?

_____

4. 16 marbles   4 sacks

How many marbles in each sack?

_____

5. Number Sense Could you divide 14 shirts into two equal groups?
Why or why not?

_____

_____

Name_____

Division as Sharing

Use counters or draw a picture to solve.

1. 3 bicycles   6 wheels

   How many wheels are on each bicycle? _____

2. 12 tennis balls   4 canisters

   How many tennis balls are in each canister? _____

3. 16 bananas   4 bunches

   How many bananas are in each bunch? _____

4. **Number Sense** One box contains 12 granola bars. Two bars are in each package. How many packages are in each box of granola bars? _____

5. Isabella and her 5 friends went to a concert at the school. They spent a total of $42 for the tickets. Each ticket was the same price. How much was each ticket? _____

6. In a yearbook club, a teacher gave out 3 new folders to each student. The teacher gave out 27 folders in all. How many students are in the yearbook club? _____

Test Prep

7. Which is the quotient of 20 ÷ 5?

   A. 2   **B.** 3   **C.** 4   **D.** 5

8. **Writing in Math** Tanya and her family went out for frozen yogurt. They ordered 10 scoops of frozen yogurt. Every person received 2 scoops. Explain how to find the number of people in Tanya's family. Then write the answer.

   _____

Name_____

Division as Repeated Subtraction

You can also think of division as repeated subtraction. Here is an example:

Joe has 15 sweaters. He is packing them into boxes. Each box holds 3 sweaters. How many boxes does Joe need?

Start with 15 sweaters. Subtract 3 at a time until there are no sweaters left. Then count the subtractions.

$15 - 3 = 12$

$12 - 3 = 9$

$9 - 3 = 6$

$6 - 3 = 3$

$3 - 3 = 0$

I can subtract three 5 times. Then there are zero sweaters left over.

You can also use division.
$15 \div 3 = 5$
Fifteen divided by 3 equals 5.
Joe needs 5 boxes.

Use counters or draw a picture to solve.

1. 10 markers   5 markers in each box

   How many boxes? _____

2. 20 books   5 books on each shelf

   How many shelves? _____

3. 8 hamsters   2 hamsters in each cage

   How many cages? _____

4. **Writing in Math** Show how you can use repeated subtraction to find how many groups of 3 are in 18. Then write the division sentence for the problem.

   _____

   _____

   _____

Division as Repeated Subtraction

Use counters or draw a picture to solve.

1. 35 stickers

5 stickers on each sheet

How many sheets?

_____

2. 40 leaves

4 leaves painted on each vase

How many vases?

_____

On Mackinac Island in Michigan, people rent bicycles because no cars are allowed on the island. The table shows the number of people who rode tandem bicycles each month. Two people ride on each tandem bicycle. How many bicycles were rented each month?

People Renting Tandem Bicycles

Month	People
May	8
June	24
July	16
August	22
September	14

3. May _____

4. June _____

5. July _____

6. August _____

7. How many bicycles were rented in all? _____

Test Prep

8. Keisha has to carry 24 boxes to her room. She can carry 3 boxes on each trip. How many trips will she take?

A. 7 trips   **B.** 8 trips   **C.** 9 trips   **D.** 10 trips

9. Writing in Math Tamara says that $15 \div 3 = 5$. Is she correct? Explain how you know.

_____

_____

Writing Division Stories

How to write a division story:

First, look at the number sentence given. Think of a situation in which the larger number is divided by the smaller number. For example, with the number sentence $20 \div 2 = n$, you might think of 20 dollars divided between 2 friends. Here is a division story for $20 \div 2 = n$:

> Dan's father gave him $20 for cutting the grass and doing other chores around the house. Since Dan's friend Steve helped him, Dan decided to divide the money by 2. How much did each boy receive?

Write a division story for each. Then use counters or draw a picture to solve.

1. $15 \div 3 = n$

_____

_____

_____

2. $12 \div 2 = n$

_____

_____

_____

3. Number Sense Sheila wrote a story problem. In her story, she asked how many equal groups 16 flowers could be put in. What does she need to tell about the groups?

_____

_____

_____

Writing Division Stories

Write a division story for each number sentence.
Then use counters or draw a picture to solve.

1. $54 \div 6 = \boxed{}$

_____

_____

_____

2. $36 \div 9 = x$

_____

_____

_____

In Colonial times, people held quilting bees. During a quilting bee, people would get together and work to make quilts. Suppose each person brought the same number of pieces of cloth to make the quilt.

Size of Quilt

Pieces of Cloth	Twin	Full	Queen
	50	77	108

3. If 10 people come to the quilting bee, how many pieces would each person need to bring to make a twin-size quilt?

_____

4. What size quilt can the people make if 9 people each bring 12 pieces of cloth?

_____

Test Prep

5. If you have 21 ice cubes, and 7 ice cubes are in each cup of juice, how many cups do you need?

A. 2 cups   **B.** 3 cups   **C.** 4 cups   **D.** 5 cups

6. **Writing in Math** Copy and finish the story shown for $22 \div 2$. Use counters or draw a picture to find the answer. Then write your own division story for $22 \div 2$.

> Justin has 22 ■. He wants to put 2 ■ in each group. How many groups will there be?

_____

_____

PROBLEM-SOLVING STRATEGY   **R 7-4**

Try, Check, and Revise

New Pencils Stephanie needs 15 pencils for school. Pencils come in packs of 4, 5, or 6. If she wants to buy 3 equal-sized packs of pencils, what size pack of pencils should she buy?

Read and Understand

Step 1: What do you know? She needs 15 pencils. Pencils come in packs of 4, 5, or 6.

Step 2: What are you trying to find? Find what size pack she needs to buy to have 3 equal-sized packs.

Plan and Solve

Step 3: What strategy will you use? Try, check, and revise

Try: packs of 4

Check: $4 + 4 + 4 = 12$ Too low

Revise: packs of 5

Check: $5 + 5 + 5 = 15$ That's it!

Look Back and Check

Step 4: Is your answer reasonable? Yes, 3 packs of 5 pencils equal 15 pencils.

Solve. Write each answer in a sentence.

1. There are 12 fish in Zack's aquarium. He has 2 kinds of fish: guppies and tetras. He has 4 more guppies than tetras. How many of each kind of fish does he have?

    _____

2. The sum of two numbers is 33. Both numbers are less than 20. The numbers are 3 apart. What are the numbers?

    _____

Name_____

Try, Check, and Revise

Solve. Write each answer in a sentence.

1. Olivia has 16 slices of bread and 2 rolls. How many sandwiches can she make?

   _____

2. Benjamin has 18 video games and 4 board games. He buys two new video games. How many games does he have in all?

   _____

3. Savannah is making a flower arrangement. She can choose 12 roses. She can choose equal amounts of 4 different colors. How many of each color can she choose?

   _____

4. Christian went fishing today for 2 hr. He caught 3 fish in the first hour he was fishing. He caught the same number of fish the second hour. He caught 2 more fish yesterday than he caught today. How many fish did he catch yesterday?

   _____

5. Four lines are drawn on a piece of paper. The third line is blue. The line above the blue line is red. The fourth line is orange. The first line is yellow. What color is the second line?

   _____

6. **Writing in Math** Ms. Ricardo has 21 students in her class. She has 5 tables in the classroom. If all of the students sit at the tables, will there be an equal number of students at each table? Explain.

   _____

   _____

Name_____

Relating Multiplication and Division

You can use what you know about multiplication to understand division. Fact families show how multiplication and division are related.

Here is the fact family for 3, 8, and 24:

$3 \times 8 = 24$ $24 \div 3 = 8$

$8 \times 3 = 24$ $24 \div 8 = 3$

factor × factor = product   dividend ÷ divisor = quotient

Complete. Use counters or draw a picture to solve.

1. $3 \times$ _____ $= 6$

   $6 \div 3 =$ _____

2. $7 \times$ _____ $= 14$

   $14 \div 7 =$ _____

3. $5 \times$ _____ $= 20$

   $20 \div 5 =$ _____

4. $4 \times$ _____ $= 24$

   $24 \div 4 =$ _____

5. **Number Sense** What other number is a part of this fact family? 3, 4, _____

6. There are 28 days in 4 weeks. What fact family would you use to find the number of days in 1 week?

   _____

7. There are 12 in. in 1 ft. What fact family would you use to find the number of inches in 2 ft?

   _____

Relating Multiplication and Division   P 7-5

Complete. Use counters or draw a picture to help.

1. $4 \times$ _____ $= 20$ **2.** $8 \times$ _____ $= 56$

$20 \div 4 =$ _____ $56 \div 8 =$ _____

3. $9 \times$ _____ $= 72$ **4.** $7 \times$ _____ $= 42$

$72 \div 9 =$ _____ $42 \div 7 =$ _____

5. $6 \times$ _____ $= 54$ **6.** $2 \times$ _____ $= 10$

$54 \div 6 =$ _____ $10 \div 2 =$ _____

7. Number Sense Write a fact family for 3, 6, and 18.

_____

_____

8. Patrick purchased 8 books at the resale shop.
He needed 4 books for each of his projects at
school. How many projects did he have? _____

Test Prep

9. A copy store charges $10 for 100 copies on white paper
and $15 for 100 copies on colored paper. Kaylee paid $40
for 300 copies. How many copies were on colored paper?

A. 100 copies   **B.** 200 copies   **C.** 300 copies   **D.** 500 copies

10. Writing in Math Evan told his class that the people in his
family have 14 legs altogether. Quinton said Evan must
have 7 people in his family. Is Quinton correct? Explain why
or why not.

_____

_____

Name_____

Dividing with 2 and 5

Thinking about multiplication can help you divide with 2 and 5.

For example:

Darren and Molly have 16 pieces of construction paper for their project. Each person will get the same number of pieces of construction paper. How many pieces will each person get?

What You **Think**	What You **Write**
Find $16 \div 2$. 2 times what number equals 16? $2 \times 8 = 16$	$16 \div 2 = 8$ So, each person will get 8 pieces of construction paper.

Solve.

1. $30 \div 5 =$ _____

2. $12 \div 2 =$ _____

3. $35 \div 5 =$ _____

4. $16 \div 2 =$ _____

5. Number Sense Write a fact family that would help you solve $15 \div 5 = n$.

_____

6. How many nickels equal one quarter? _____ What multiplication fact can you use to help solve this problem?

_____

7. How many dimes equal one half-dollar? _____ What multiplication fact can you use to help solve this problem?

_____

8. How many quarters equal one half-dollar? _____

Coins	
Penny	1 cent
Nickel	5 cents
Dime	10 cents
Quarter	25 cents
Half-dollar	50 cents

Dividing with 2 and 5

1. 20 ÷ 5 = _____   **2.** 16 ÷ 2 = _____   **3.** 12 ÷ 2 = _____

4. 40 ÷ 5 = _____   **5.** 25 ÷ 5 = _____   **6.** 8 ÷ 2 = _____

7. 30 ÷ 5 = _____   **8.** 10 ÷ 2 = _____   **9.** 15 ÷ 5 = _____

10. Find 45 ÷ 5. _____   **11.** Divide 14 by 2. _____

12. Number Sense Explain how you can use multiplication to help you find 20 ÷ 5.

_____

_____

13. A wolf spider has 8 eyes and 8 legs. How many spiders would there be if there were 16 eyes and 16 legs?

_____

14. William has 1 quarter, 2 dimes, and 1 nickel. Abigail has $0.10 more than William and has only nickels. How many nickels does Abigail have?

_____

15. Gabriella and 4 friends shared a pack of 15 gluesticks equally. How many gluesticks did each person get?

_____

Test Prep

16. John has 25 colored pencils. If John equally divides the pencils between 5 people, how many pencils will each person get?

A. 2 pencils   **B.** 4 pencils   **C.** 5 pencils   **D.** 7 pencils

17. Writing in Math Franklin says that if he divides 50 by 5, he will get 10. Jeff says he should get 9. Who is correct? Explain.

_____

_____

© Pearson Education, Inc. 3

Name_____

Dividing with 3 and 4

R 7-7

You can use multiplication facts for 3 and 4 to help you divide by 3 or 4.

Problem	Peter has 32 planks. If he places them in four equal piles, how many planks will be in each pile?	May and her two friends have 21 treats. If each person gets an equal amount, how many treats does each girl get?
What You **Think**	Four times what number equals 32? $4 \times 8 = 32$	Three times what number equals 21? $3 \times 7 = 21$
What You **Write**	$32 \div 4 = 8$ There will be 8 planks in each pile.	$21 \div 3 = 7$ Each girl gets 7 treats.

You can write a division problem in two ways:

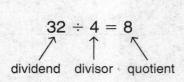   **or**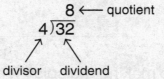

---

1. $30 \div 3 =$ _____

2. $20 \div 4 =$ _____

3. $15 \div 3 =$ _____

4. $4\overline{)40}$

5. $3\overline{)18}$

6. $4\overline{)28}$

7. Number Sense What multiplication fact could help you find $27 \div 3$?

_____

8. Ms. Johnson's class has 24 students. Could Ms. Johnson place her class into 3 equal-sized groups? _____

9. How many students would be in each of the 3 groups? _____

© Pearson Education, Inc. 3

Name_____

Dividing with 3 and 4

1. 9 ÷ 3 = _____   **2.** 40 ÷ 4 = _____   **3.** 21 ÷ 3 = _____

4. 32 ÷ 4 = _____   **5.** 30 ÷ 3 = _____   **6.** 18 ÷ 3 = _____

7. 20 ÷ 4 = _____   **8.** 24 ÷ 3 = _____   **9.** 36 ÷ 4 = _____

10. 4)$\overline{28}$ **11.** 3)$\overline{15}$ **12.** 4)$\overline{16}$

13. Divide 27 by 3. _____   **14.** Find 32 divided by 4. _____

15. Number Sense Explain how you can use 4 × 5 = 20 to find 20 ÷ 4.

_____

_____

16. The third-grade class is making a display for science. The poster board they are using is 36 in. long. The teacher needs to cut it into 3 equal pieces. How long will each piece be? _____

Test Prep

17. Which is the quotient of 40 ÷ 4?

A. 7   **B.** 8   **C.** 9   **D.** 10

18. Writing in Math Wendell has a box with 32 cherries. He shares the cherries equally with 3 friends. Bonnie received 7 cherries. She thinks she should have one more. Is she correct? Explain.

_____

_____

_____

Name_____

Dividing with 6 and 7

When you divide, you separate things into equal groups.

> For example:
>
> Find 35 ÷ 7.

There are 35 circles.   Divide them into   There are 5 circles
                          7 equal groups.   in each group.
                                               So 35 ÷ 7 = 5

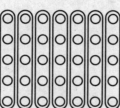

---

1. 30 ÷ 6 = _____   **2.** 28 ÷ 7 = _____   **3.** 42 ÷ 6 = _____

4. 7)‾49   **5.** 6)‾24   **6.** 6)‾12

7. Number Sense Name a number that can be equally
divided into groups of 6 and groups of 7.   _____

There are several different ways a football team
can score points. Two of the ways are shown
in the table.

Play	Points
Touchdown	6
Touchdown with extra point	7

8. If a football team has scored 3 times and
has a total of 18 points, how did they score
each time?

_____

9. If a football team has scored 3 times and has a total of
19 points, how did they score each time?

_____

_____

Name_____

Dicviding with 6 and 7

1. $36 \div 6 =$ _____

2. $42 \div 6 =$ _____

3. $70 \div 7 =$ _____

4. $60 \div 6 =$ _____

5. $56 \div 7 =$ _____

6. $49 \div 7 =$ _____

7. $6 \div 6 =$ _____

8. $28 \div 7 =$ _____

9. $18 \div 6 =$ _____

10. $6\overline{)24}$

11. $7\overline{)35}$

12. $6\overline{)30}$

13. Divide 12 by 6. _____

14. Find 42 divided by 7. _____

15. **Number Sense** How many groups of 6 are there in 36? Explain how you know.

_____

_____

16. Connor has 48 apples. He separated the apples equally into 6 crates. How many apples are there in each crate?   _____

17. Sierra's karate class lasts 56 days. How many weeks does the class last?   _____

Test Prep

18. Jada's third-grade class is leaving on a field trip. There are 32 people going on the field trip. The group will ride in vans that each hold 8 people. How many vans will the class need?

    A. 4 vans   **B.** 5 vans   **C.** 6 vans   **D.** 7 vans

19. **Writing in Math** Kyle says there are exactly 4 weeks in February. Is he right? Explain.

_____

_____

Dividing with 8 and 9

Remembering multiplication facts can help you divide by 8 and 9.

What multiplication fact can help you find 24 ÷ 8?

8 x 1 = 8	8 x 6 = 48
8 x 2 = 16	8 x 7 = 56
(8 x 3 = 24)	8 x 8 = 64
8 x 4 = 32	8 x 9 = 72
8 x 5 = 40	8 x 10 = 80

If $8 \times 3 = 24$, then $24 \div 8 = 3$.

What multiplication fact can help you find 27 ÷ 9?

9 x 1 = 9	9 x 6 = 54
9 x 2 = 18	9 x 7 = 63
(9 x 3 = 27)	9 x 8 = 72
9 x 4 = 36	9 x 9 = 81
9 x 5 = 45	9 x 10 = 90

If $9 \times 3 = 27$, then $27 \div 9 = 3$.

---

1. 32 ÷ 8 = _____   **2.** 54 ÷ 9 = _____   **3.** 48 ÷ 8 = _____

4. 9)‾72‾   **5.** 9)‾63‾   **6.** 8)‾56‾

7. Number Sense What multiplication fact could
you use to find a number that can be divided
equally by 8 and by 9?

_____

8. From 1912 until the beginning of 1959, the United
States had 48 states. The flag at that time had
48 stars, one for each state. The 48 stars on the
flag were arranged in 6 equal rows. How many
stars were in each row?

_____

Name_____

Dividing with 8 and 9

1. $27 \div 9 =$ _____
2. $45 \div 9 =$ _____
3. $72 \div 8 =$ _____

4. $81 \div 9 =$ _____
5. $24 \div 8 =$ _____
6. $63 \div 9 =$ _____

7. $64 \div 8 =$ _____
8. $36 \div 9 =$ _____
9. $48 \div 8 =$ _____

10. $9\overline{)18}$
11. $8\overline{)40}$
12. $9\overline{)72}$

13. Find 16 divided by 8. _____
14. Divide 90 by 9. _____

15. **Number Sense** What multiplication fact can help you find $32 \div 8$?

_____

_____

16. Nicholas scored 16 runs in the first 8 baseball games
he played. If he scored the same number of times in
each game, how many runs did he score in each game? _____

Test Prep

17. Mr. Carlos brought 32 pencils to school. He shared them
equally among the 8 students in the math group. How
many pencils did each student get?

    A. 2 pencils   **B.** 3 pencils   **C.** 4 pencils   **D.** 5 pencils

18. **Writing in Math** Adam made 19 paper cranes on Monday
and 8 on Tuesday. He gave 9 of his friends an equal
number of cranes. How many did each friend receive?
Explain how you found your answer.

_____

_____

Name

Dividing with 0 and 1

There are special rules to follow when dividing by 1 or 0.

Rule	Example	What You **Think**	What You **Write**
When any number is divided by 1, the quotient is that number.	$7 \div 1 = ?$	1 times what number = 7? $1 \times 7 = 7$ So, $7 \div 1 = 7$	$7 \div 1 = 7$ or $1\overline{)7}$ with quotient 7
When any number (except 0) is divided by itself, the quotient is 1.	$8 \div 8 = ?$	8 times what number = 8? $8 \times 1 = 8$ So, $8 \div 8 = 1$	$8 \div 8 = 1$ or $8\overline{)8}$ with quotient 1
When zero is divided by a number (except 0), the quotient is 0.	$0 \div 5 = ?$	5 times what number = 0? $5 \times 0 = 0$ So, $0 \div 5 = 0$	$0 \div 5 = 0$ or $5\overline{)0}$ with quotient 0
You cannot divide a number by 0.	$9 \div 0 = ?$	0 times what number = 9? There is no number that works, so $9 \div 0$ cannot be done.	$9 \div 0$ cannot be done

1. $25 \div 1 =$ _____

2. $9 \div 9 =$ _____

3. $0 \div 8 =$ _____

4. $1\overline{)7}$

5. $12\overline{)12}$

6. $0\overline{)17}$

Compare. Use $<$, $>$, or $=$.

7. $15 \div 1 \bigcirc 15 \div 15$

8. $0 \div 12 \bigcirc 12 \div 12$

9. $8 \div 1 \bigcirc 8 \div 1$

10. $1 \div 1 \bigcirc 0 \div 1$

Dividing with 0 and 1

1. $9 \div 1 =$ _____   **2.** $0 \div 8 =$ _____   **3.** $7 \div 7 =$ _____

4. $0 \div 9 =$ _____   **5.** $3 \div 3 =$ _____   **6.** $6 \div 1 =$ _____

7. $1\overline{)3}$ **8.** $4\overline{)4}$ **9.** $8\overline{)0}$

10. Divide 0 by 2. _____   **11.** Divide 7 by 1. _____

12. Number Sense Explain how you know that $45 \div 0$ cannot be done.

_____

_____

Compare. Use $<$, $>$, or $=$.

13. $6 \div 6 \bigcirc 4 \div 4$ **14.** $0 \div 5 \bigcirc 5 \div 5$ **15.** $10 \div 1 \bigcirc 7 \div 1$

Test Prep

16. Which is the quotient of $0 \div 9$?

    A. 9   **B.** 5

    C. 1   **D.** 0

17. Writing in Math Explain why $10 - 0 = 10$ but $0 \div 10 = 0$.

_____

_____

_____

_____

Remainders

Keith has 21 sports cards. Each plastic sleeve holds 6 cards. How many sleeves will be filled? Will there be any cards left over?

Find 21 ÷ 6.

What You **Do**	What You **Write**
Draw a picture to show the main idea of the problem. 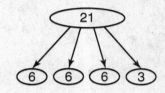 There are 3 groups of 6 with 3 left over. The remainder is 3.	21 ÷ 6 = 3 R3 3 R3 is read "three remainder three." Keith filled 3 sleeves. He has 3 cards left over.

Use counters or draw a picture to find each quotient and remainder.

1. 16 ÷ 5 = _____

2. 14 ÷ 3 = _____

3. 19 ÷ 8 = _____

4. 17 ÷ 4 = _____

5. 8 ÷ 3 = _____

6. 11 ÷ 7 = _____

7. Number Sense Jamal divided 16 by 5. His answer was 2 R6. Is his answer correct? If not, what is the correct answer?

_____

There are 50 states in the United States. Mr. Hernandez's students are going to study each state.

8. Mr. Hernandez has assigned a group of 8 students to write paragraphs about the states. If the group of 8 students needs to write a paragraph about each of the 50 states, can the work be divided evenly among the students in the group? _____

If not, how many states are left over? _____

Remainders

Use counters or draw a picture to find each quotient and remainder.

1. 39 ÷ 6 = _____   **2.** 20 ÷ 3 = _____   **3.** 11 ÷ 3 = _____

4. 9 ÷ 2 = _____   **5.** 7 ÷ 3 = _____   **6.** 13 ÷ 6 = _____

7. 36 ÷ 3 = _____   **8.** 25 ÷ 4 = _____   **9.** 45 ÷ 6 = _____

10. Holly bought a box of 65 souvenir magnets on her vacation. She wants to share them equally with her 9 friends. How many magnets will each friend get? How many magnets will be left over?

_____

11. Sebastian and Caitlin have 11 thank-you cards to send. They agreed that if each of them sends 5 they will be finished. Do you agree? Explain.

_____

Test Prep

12. Yvonne can carry 7 books at one time, and she wants to carry 25 books to her room. How many books will she carry on her fourth trip?

A. 1 book   **B.** 2 books   **C.** 3 books   **D.** 4 books

13. Writing in Math Anna has 30 fruit snacks that she wants to share with her class. Because there are 25 people in her class, Anna used 30 ÷ 25 to find the number of snacks she will have left over. Will she find the correct answer? Explain.

_____

_____

_____

Name_____

Division Patterns with 10, 11, and 12 ^{R 7-12}

A number is divisible by another number when it can be divided by that number and the remainder is 0. For example, $80 \div 10 = 8$. You can also say that 80 is a **multiple** of 10. The chart below shows the multiples of 10, 11, and 12.

×	0	1	2	3	4	5	6	7	8	9	10	11	12
0	0	0	0	0	0	0	0	0	0	0	0	0	0
1	0	1	2	3	4	5	6	7	8	9	10	11	12
2	0	2	4	6	8	10	12	14	16	18	20	22	24
3	0	3	6	9	12	15	18	21	24	27	30	33	36
4	0	4	8	12	16	20	24	28	32	36	40	44	48
5	0	5	10	15	20	25	30	35	40	45	50	55	60
6	0	6	12	18	24	30	36	42	48	54	60	66	72
7	0	7	14	21	28	35	42	49	56	63	70	77	84
8	0	8	16	24	32	40	48	56	64	72	80	88	96
9	0	9	18	27	36	45	54	63	72	81	90	99	108
10	0	10	20	30	40	50	60	70	80	90	100	110	120
11	0	11	22	33	44	55	66	77	88	99	110	121	132
12	0	12	24	36	48	60	72	84	96	108	120	132	144

- The numbers 0, 10, 20, …, 120 are all multiples of 10. Each of these numbers is divisible by 10. For example, $30 \div 10 = 3$.

- The numbers 0, 11, 22, …, 132 are all multiples of 11. Each of these numbers is divisible by 11. For example, $99 \div 11 = 9$.

- The numbers 0, 12, 24, …, 144 are all multiples of 12. Each of these numbers is divisible by 12. For example, $108 \div 12 = 9$.

Find each quotient. You may use a multiplication table, counters, or draw a picture to help.

1. $48 \div 12 =$ _____   **2.** $50 \div 10 =$ _____   **3.** $44 \div 11 =$ _____

4. $11\overline{)66}$ **5.** $10\overline{)20}$ **6.** $12\overline{)48}$

7. Writing in Math Explain how you can use skip counting to find $70 \div 10$.

_____

_____

Name_____

Division Patterns with 10, 11, and 12 ^{P 7-12}

Find each quotient. You may use a multiplication table,
counters, or draw a picture to help.

1. $121 \div 11 =$ _____   **2.** $70 \div 7 =$ _____   **3.** $132 \div 11 =$ _____

4. $72 \div 12 =$ _____   **5.** $66 \div 6 =$ _____   **6.** $40 \div 4 =$ _____

7. $300 \div 30 =$ _____   **8.** $22 \div 2 =$ _____   **9.** $200 \div 10 =$ _____

10. $8\overline{)88}$ **11.** $9\overline{)36}$ **12.** $10\overline{)110}$

13. Number Sense Adrian said that any 2-digit number with
2 identical digits is divisible by 11. Do you agree? Explain.

_____

_____

14. Madeline purchased 10 sweaters for $100.
How much did she spend for each sweater? _____

Test Prep

15. Henry bought 4 dozen eggs. How many eggs did he buy?

A. 48 eggs   **B.** 60 eggs   **C.** 72 eggs   **D.** 84 eggs

16. Writing in Math Explain how you can find the quotient of $400 \div 10$.

_____

_____

_____

94 Use with Lesson 7-12.

PROBLEM-SOLVING SKILL

Translating Words to Expressions

Family Kay has 5 fewer aunts than cousins. She has 15 cousins. Write a numerical expression that shows how many aunts and cousins Kay has total.

The words in the problem give you clues about the operation.

Word or Phrase	Use
Total	+
Difference of	−
Times	×
Half; placed into equal groups	÷

Since Kay has 15 cousins, and 5 fewer aunts than cousins, she must have 10 aunts. The numerical expression that shows the total number of aunts and cousins she has is 10 + 15.

Write the numerical expression for each word phrase.

1. 14 baseball cards placed into 2 equal groups   _____

2. 12 more than 85   _____

3. 6 times as long as 7   _____

4. 3 times as old as 5   _____

5. the total of 4 cats and 15 dogs   _____

6. $14 less than $44   _____

7. Writing in Math Write a word phrase for this numerical expression: 8 × 5.

_____

_____

Name_____

Translating Words to Expressions

Write a numerical expression for each word phrase.

1. 42 minus 10 baseballs   _____

2. four times as many crayons as 4 colored pencils   _____

3. $9 less than $25   _____

4. 15 toys given out equally to 5 students   _____

5. 12 times as long as 2 in.   _____

6. 4 people sharing 8 rolls equally   _____

There are 12 cups in one package. Write a numerical expression
for how many there will be when there are

7. 2 fewer cups.   _____

8. 8 more cups.   _____

9. 6 times as many cups.   _____

10. half the number of cups.   _____

Choose the numerical expression that matches the situation.

11. Karl eats all 5 of his carrots.   **12.** Both cats receive 10 oz of food.

   A. $5 + 5$ **A.** $10 \div 2$

   B. $5 - 5$ **B.** 10×2

13. Writing in Math Write two situations that would use the
numerical expression $27 \div 9$.

_____

_____

_____

© Pearson Education, Inc. 3

PROBLEM-SOLVING APPLICATION   **R 7-14**

The Student Musicians

The fifth- and sixth-grade string music students at Highland Elementary gave a concert. Several different groups of student musicians played songs. One of the groups had 4 members. Their instruments had a total of 20 strings. What instruments could these group members be playing?

String Instruments

Instrument	Number of Strings
Violin	4
Viola	4
Cello	4
Bass	4
Guitar	6

Try: First, try 1 guitar and 3 violins.

Check: 3 violins × 4 strings each = 12 strings, plus 6 guitar strings equals 18 strings. This answer is too low by 2 strings.

Revise: I'll try 2 violins and 2 guitars. This should give me 20 strings. 4 × 2 = 8, 6 × 2 = 12, 12 + 8 = 20.

This answer works. I have 4 string players and 20 strings.

---

1. There are a total of 32 string players in the fifth and sixth grades. There are 6 more fifth graders than sixth graders. How many string players are in each grade?

   _____

2. The 32 string players often play in groups of 4 players. How many groups of 4 players could they form?

   _____

3. If the string players are divided into groups of 6 players, are

   there any students left over? _____ If so, how many? _____

4. The string players played a concert that included 5 songs. The songs were all the same length. The concert lasted 30 min. How long was each song?

   _____

Name_____

The Dividing Life

Solve. Write your answer in a complete sentence.

1. Bailey is collecting dimes. She has 4 quarters. If Bailey changes her quarters for dimes at the bank, how many dimes will she get?

_____

2. At the zoo, there are 8 elephants and 2 trainers. How many elephants does each trainer work with if they both work with the same number of elephants?

_____

3. There are 16 oz in a pound of butter. While making bread, Andre read that he needs half that amount for the recipe. How many ounces does Andre need?

_____

4. Thomas has 3 boxes for toys in his room. He has 33 toys. If he divides the toys equally, how many toys will Thomas put into each box?

_____

5. Makayla has 32 books. She let each of her 4 friends borrow the same number of books. They borrowed all of Makayla's books. How many books did each friend borrow?

_____

6. Ms. Lucas has 19 paintbrushes for art class and 4 tables. If she puts an equal number of brushes on each table, how many brushes will be on each table? How many brushes will be left over?

_____

_____

Name_____

Solid Figures

Three-dimensional objects are called solid figures. Solid figures are found in the world in many shapes and sizes.

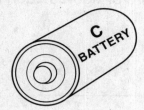
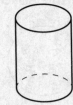

The battery is an example of a cylinder. A **solid figure** is named according to its features.

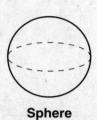

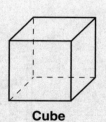
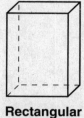
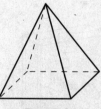

| Sphere | Cone | Cube | Rectangular Prism | Pyramid |

Name the solid figure or figures each object looks like.

1.

_____

2.

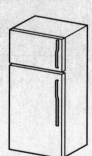

_____

3.

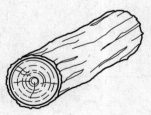

_____

4.

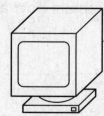

_____

Name_____

Solid Figures

Name the solid figure or figures each object looks like.

1.

_____

2.

_____

3.

_____

4.

_____

5. What solid figures would you get if you cut a cube as shown?

_____

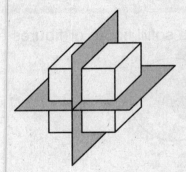

Test Prep

6. Which has the most flat surfaces?

A. Pyramid   **B.** Cylinder   **C.** Cone   **D.** Rectangular prism

7. Writing in Math Explain how a pyramid and a cone are alike and different.

_____

_____

_____

Name_____

Relating Solids and Shapes

In a drawing of a solid figure, it is not always easy to find the number of faces, edges, or corners. Sometimes it helps to imagine that the solid figure is transparent.

By using a transparent cube, you can count each face. Remember that each flat surface is called a **face.**

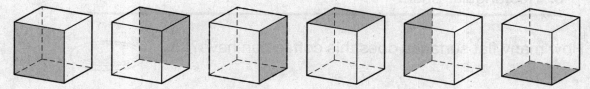

There are 6 faces on a cube.

Use the transparent cube to count the number of edges. Remember that an **edge** is a line segment where two faces meet. There are 12 edges on a cube.

Can you use the transparent cube to find the number of corners on a cube? Remember a **corner** is the point where 2 or more edges meet. There are 8 corners on a cube.

1. How many faces does a rectangular prism have? _____

2. How many edges does a pyramid have? _____

3. How many corners does a rectangular prism have? _____

4. **Reasoning** How are a cube and a rectangular prism alike? How are they different?

_____

_____

_____

_____

Name_____

Relating Solids and Shapes

Complete the table.

Solid Figure	Faces	Edges	Corners
1. Cube			
2. Pyramid			
3. Rectangular prism			

4. How many flat surfaces does this coffee can have?

_____

Jane is making a building for her math project. How many corners does each combination of figures have?

5. 2 rectangular prisms _____

6. 2 pyramids _____

7. 2 cubes and 1 cylinder _____

Test Prep

8. Which figure is NOT part of this object?

A. Sphere   B. Cylinder

C. Cone   D. Cube

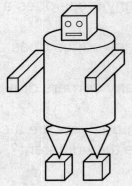

9. **Writing in Math** How could you describe a cylinder to someone who has never seen one?

_____

_____

_____

_____

Name_____

PROBLEM-SOLVING STRATEGY

Act It Out

R 8-3

Bricks Jacob wants to know how many bricks there are in the stack, and he knows the stack is completely filled. How many bricks are in the stack?

Read and Understand

Step 1: What do you know? The bottom layer of bricks is 3 bricks wide and 3 bricks long. The middle layer of bricks is 2 bricks wide and 2 bricks long. There is one brick on the top.

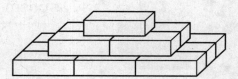

Step 2: What are you trying to find? The total number of bricks in the stack

Plan and Solve

Step 3: What strategy will you use?   **Strategy:** Act it out

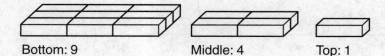

Bottom: 9   Middle: 4   Top: 1

$9 + 4 + 1 = 14$ Answer: There are a total of 14 bricks in the stack.

Look Back and Check

Step 4: Is your answer reasonable? Yes. The bottom layer has 9, the middle layer has 4, and the top layer has 1 brick.

---

1. When the wall has been built up to the fifth layer, how many cylinder-shaped blocks will have been used?

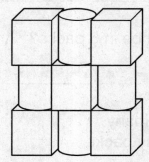

© Pearson Education, Inc. 3

Name_____

Act It Out

Solve each problem by acting it out. Write the answer in
a complete sentence.

Kate built the 3 houses below with her building blocks.
How many blocks did she use for each house?

1.

_____

2.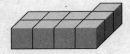

_____

3.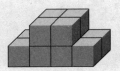

_____

Jamie and Peter are playing a rhythm game. Every time Jamie
claps his hands, Peter stomps his feet twice.

4. After Jamie has clapped his hands 8 times, how many
   times has Peter stomped his feet?

_____

5. If Peter stomps his feet 12 times, how many times does
   Jamie clap his hands?

_____

6. If pencils were sold 4 to a pack, how many would be in 6 packs?

_____

7. **Decision Making** You are going to buy twice as many
   pencils as someone who has 8 pencils. How many packs
   of pencils will you buy?

_____

Lines and Line Segments

You can find lines and parts of lines in shapes and objects.

		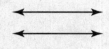		
A **line** is a set of points that is endless in both directions. Lines have arrows on each end.	A **line segment** is part of a line. It has an endpoint on each end.	A **ray** is part of a line that is endless in one direction. A ray has an endpoint on one end and an arrow on the other.	**Parallel lines** never cross. They also stay the same distance apart from one another.	**Intersecting lines** cross at one point. Any lines that are not parallel are intersecting.

Write the name for each.

1.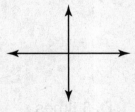

_____

2.

_____

3.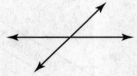

_____

4.

_____

5.

_____

6.

_____

7. Reasoning Is it possible for two rays to be parallel to each other? _____

Name_____

Lines and Line Segments

Write the name for each.

1.

_____

2.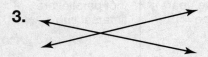

_____

3.

_____

4. Draw a set of parallel lines.

Use the map. Tell if the trails are parallel or intersecting.

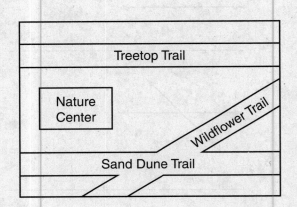

5. Treetop and Sand Dune

_____

6. Sand Dune and Wildflower

_____

Test Prep

7. How many times does a pair of intersecting lines cross?

   A. Never   **B.** 1 time   **C.** 2 times   **D.** 3 times

8. **Writing in Math** Explain how you can tell the difference between a ray and a line.

_____

_____

Angles

A **right angle** forms what is normally called a square corner. When two lines form right angles, the lines are called **perpendicular lines.**

An **acute angle** is less than a right angle.

An **obtuse angle** is greater than a right angle.

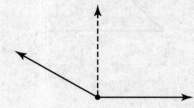

Tell whether each angle is right, acute, or obtuse.

1.

_____

2.

_____

3.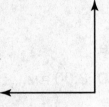

_____

4.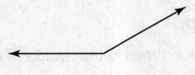

_____

Look at the capital letters and tell what kind of angle is in each letter.

5. L

_____

6. V

_____

Angles

Tell whether each angle is right, acute, or obtuse.

1.

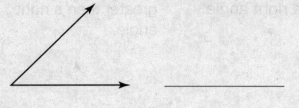

_____

2.

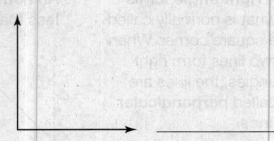

_____

3.

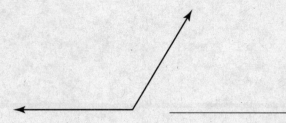

_____

4.

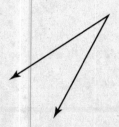

_____

5. Draw a right angle. Then draw an acute angle and an obtuse angle.

Test Prep

6. At which time do the hands of a clock form an acute angle?

   A. 2:00 P.M.   **B.** 4:00 P.M.   **C.** 6:00 P.M.   **D.** 8:00 P.M.

7. **Writing in Math** Describe an object that has a right angle.

   _____

   _____

   _____

Polygons

Polygons are closed figures that are made up of straight line segments.

Not a polygon
Not a closed
figure

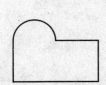

Not a polygon
Not all straight
lines

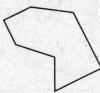

Polygon
Closed figure
All straight lines

The number of sides in a polygon gives the polygon its name.

Triangle
3 sides

Quadrilateral
4 sides

Pentagon
5 sides

Hexagon
6 sides

Octagon
8 sides

Is each figure a polygon? If it is a polygon, give its name. If not, explain why.

1.

_____

_____

2.

_____

_____

3.
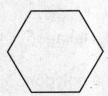

_____

_____

4.

_____

_____

Name_____

Polygons

Is each figure below a polygon? If it is a polygon, give its name.
If not, explain why.

1. 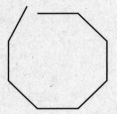   _____

2. 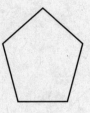   _____

Which polygon has

3. 6 sides?   _____

4. 8 sides?   _____

5. Reasoning Explain how you know the next polygon in the pattern.

_____

_____

Test Prep

6. Which is NOT a polygon?

A. Triangle   **B.** Pentagon   **C.** Circle   **D.** Hexagon

7. Writing in Math Explain why the shape of a football is not a polygon.

_____

_____

Triangles

Triangles are polygons with three sides.

Triangles can be named by the lengths of their sides.

 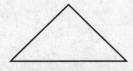 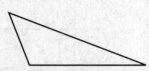

Equilateral Triangle
All sides are the same length.

Isosceles Triangle
At least two sides are the same length.

Scalene Triangle
No sides are the same length.

Triangles can also be described by their angles.

  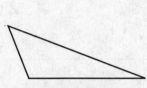

Right Triangle
One angle is a right angle.

Acute Triangle
All three angles are acute angles.

Obtuse Triangle
One angle is an obtuse angle.

Tell if the triangle is equilateral, isosceles, or scalene.

1.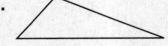

2.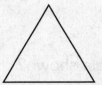

3.

_____   _____   _____

Tell if the triangle is right, acute, or obtuse.

4.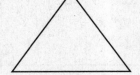

5.

6.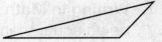

_____   _____   _____

Name_____

Triangles

Tell if each triangle is equilateral, isosceles, or scalene.

1.

_____

2.

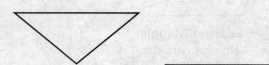

_____

Tell if each triangle is right, acute, or obtuse.

3.

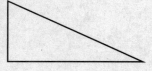   _____

4.

   _____

5. Draw an equilateral triangle.

Test Prep

6. Which best describes the triangle shown?

   A. Acute triangle, equilateral triangle

   B. Obtuse triangle, equilateral triangle

   C. Right triangle, scalene triangle

   D. Obtuse triangle, scalene triangle

7. Writing in Math Is it possible for an isosceles triangle to be an acute triangle? Explain.

_____

_____

Quadrilaterals

Special quadrilaterals can be separated into groups. The chart shows how they are defined.

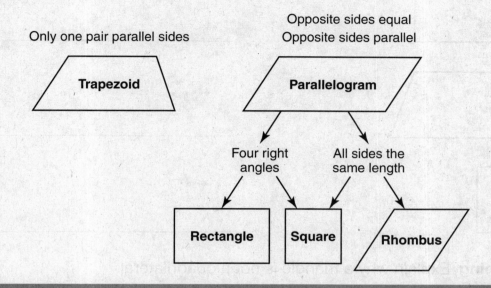

Only one pair parallel sides

Trapezoid

Opposite sides equal
Opposite sides parallel

Parallelogram

Four right angles

All sides the same length

Rectangle   **Square**   **Rhombus**

Write the name of each quadrilateral.

1.

_____

2.

_____

3.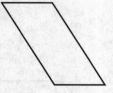

_____

4.

_____

5.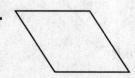

_____

6.

_____

Name_____

Quadrilaterals

Write the name of each quadrilateral.

1.

_____

2.

_____

3.

_____

4. **Reasoning** Explain why a triangle is not a quadrilateral.

_____

_____

5. Draw a quadrilateral with four equal sides, but no right
   angles. What is its name?

_____

Test Prep

6. Which of the following correctly names the figure?

   A. Rhombus   **B.** Trapezoid

   C. Parallelogram   **D.** Rectangle

7. **Writing in Math** If you turn a rhombus upside down, will it
   still be a rhombus? Explain.

_____

_____

Name _____

Congruent Figures and Motion

R 8-9

Congruent figures are figures that have the same size and the same shape.

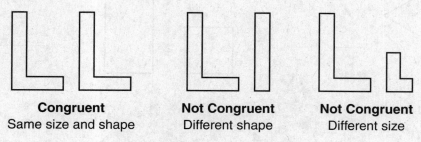

Congruent
Same size and shape

Not Congruent
Different shape

Not Congruent
Different size

Figures can be moved in a number of ways. You can slide, turn, or flip a figure without changing its size or shape.

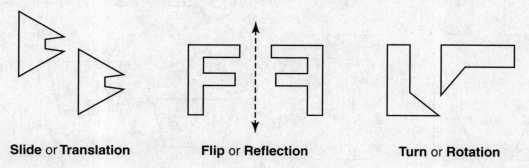

Slide or **Translation**

Flip or **Reflection**

Turn or **Rotation**

In each case, the original figure has been moved to form a new figure that is congruent to the original.

Are the figures congruent? Write *yes* or *no*.

1.

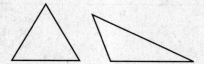

_____

2.

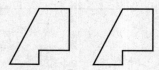

_____

Write *flip*, *slide*, or *turn* for each.

3.

_____

4.

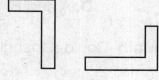

_____

© Pearson Education, Inc. 3

Use with Lesson 8-9. **105**

Name_____

Congruent Figures and Motion

Are the figures congruent? Write *yes* or *no*.

1. 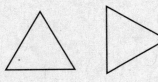 _____

2. 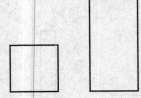 _____

Write *flip*, *slide*, or *turn* for each.

3. 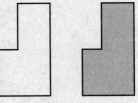 _____

4. 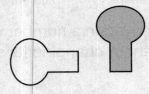 _____

5. 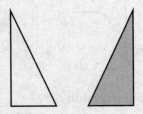 _____

6. 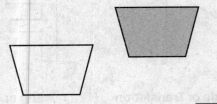 _____

7. **Reasoning** Are all squares congruent? Explain.

_____

_____

Test Prep

8. Which of the following are congruent figures?

   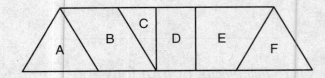

   A. A and E   **B.** B and D

   C. C and F   **D.** A and F

9. **Writing in Math** Could a triangle and a square ever be congruent? Explain.

_____

Symmetry

Figures are **symmetric** if you can divide them in half and both halves are congruent.

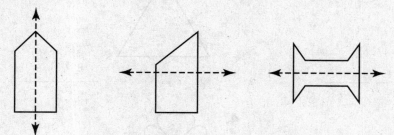

The figure is
symmetric.
The halves match.

The figure is
not symmetric.
The halves do
not match.

The figure is
symmetric.
The halves match.

A line which divides a symmetric figure is called a **line of symmetry.** Some figures have more than one line of symmetry.

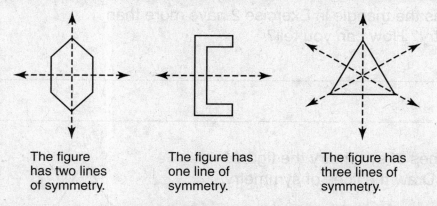

The figure
has two lines
of symmetry.

The figure has
one line of
symmetry.

The figure has
three lines of
symmetry.

Tell whether each figure is symmetric. Write *yes* or *no*.

1.

_____

2.

_____

3.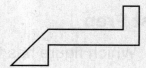

_____

4.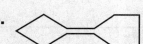

_____

5.

_____

6.

_____

Name_____

Symmetry

Tell whether each figure is symmetric. Write *yes* or *no*.

1. 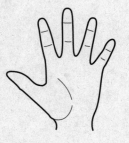 _____

2. _____

3. 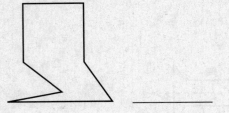 _____

4.  _____

5. **Reasoning** Does the triangle in Exercise 2 have more than 1 line of symmetry? How can you tell?

_____

_____

6. Tell how many lines of symmetry the figure at the right has. Draw the lines of symmetry.

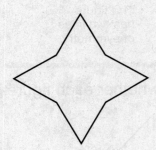

_____

Test Prep

7. Which figure has the most lines of symmetry?

A. Square   **B.** Circle   **C.** Triangle   **D.** Hexagon

8. **Writing in Math** Can a chair be symmetric? Explain.

_____

_____

_____

Perimeter

The **perimeter** of a figure is the distance around it.

The perimeter is found by adding the lengths of the sides. To find the perimeter of the figure, add the lengths.

2 ft + 2 ft + 6 ft + 2 ft + 4 ft + 1 ft +
4 ft + 2 ft + 7 ft = 30 ft

The perimeter of the figure is 30 feet.

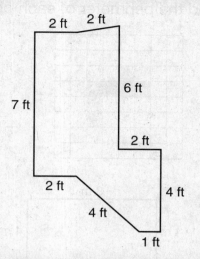

Find the perimeter of each polygon.

1. 4 in. 10 in. 12 in.

_____

2. 4 m 4 m 2 m 4 m 3 m 1 m 1 m 3 m

_____

3. 9 ft 9 ft 9 ft 9 ft

_____

4. What is the perimeter of a rectangle that is 5 yd long and 3 yd wide?

_____

5. What is the perimeter of a garden that is 20 ft long and 15 ft wide?

_____

6. What is the perimeter of a square table with a side length of 50 inches?

_____

Name_____

Perimeter

Find the perimeter of each polygon.

1. 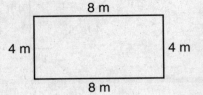   _____

2. 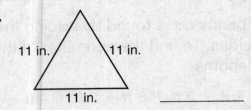   _____

3. 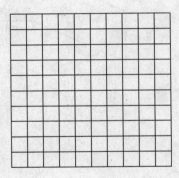   _____

4. 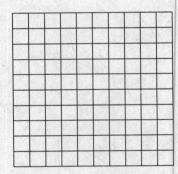   _____

Draw a figure with the given perimeter.

5. 10 units

6. 22 units

Test Prep

7. Which is the best estimate for the perimeter of your math book?

   A. 5 in.   **B.** 10 ft   **C.** 25 in.   **D.** 25 ft

8. Writing in Math Explain how you could use grid paper to draw a rectangle with a perimeter of 18 units.

_____

_____

_____

Name_____

Area

The **area** of a figure can be found in two ways.

A **square unit** is a square with sides that are each 1 unit long.

You can think of the grid squares as an array.

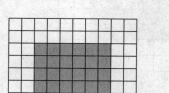

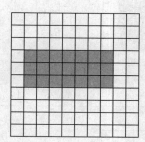

Count the square units in the shaded rectangle. Since there are 24 squares, the area of the rectangle is 24 square units.

Each row has 7 squares. To find the rectangle's area, multiply. $3 \times 7 = 21$, so the rectangle's area is 21 square units.

Find the area of each shaded figure. Write your answer in square units.

1.

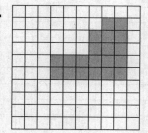

_____

2.

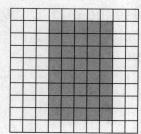

_____

3.

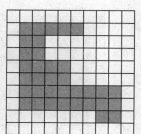

_____

4.

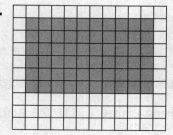

_____

© Pearson Education, Inc. 3

Name_____

Area

Find the area of each figure. Write your answer in square units.

1.
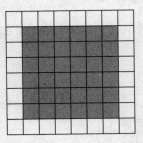

_____

2.
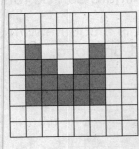

_____

3.
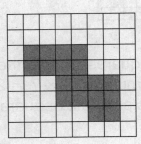

_____

4.
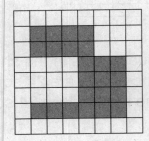

_____

5. **Reasoning** Use the grid. Draw two different figures that each have a perimeter of 14. Find each area.

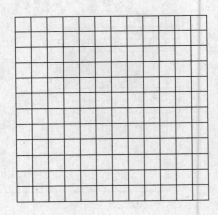

Test Prep

6. Which is the area of this figure?

   A. 27 square units   **B.** 26 square units

   C. 25 square units   **D.** 24 square units

7. **Writing in Math** Explain why it would be important to know the area of a room that new furniture will be going into.

_____

108 Use with Lesson 8-12.

Name_____

Volume

In a solid, the **volume** is the number of cubic units that are needed to fill the figure. A **cubic unit** is a cube with edges that are each 1 unit long.

The rectangular prism to the right is 2 units wide, 1 unit high, and 1 unit long.

It takes 2 cubic units to fill the rectangular prism, so the volume of the rectangular prism is 2 cubic units.

Find the volume of each figure. Write your answer in cubic units.

1.

_____

2.

_____

3.

_____

4.

_____

5.

_____

6.

_____

7. Number Sense Carl built a cube with edges that are 3 in. long. What is the volume of Carl's cube?

_____

Name_____

Volume

Find the volume of each figure. Write your answer in cubic units.

1.

_____

2.

_____

3.

_____

4.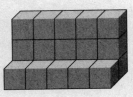

_____

5. Estimate the volume of the cube in cubic units.

_____

_____

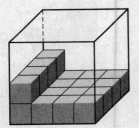

6. Kevin made a rectangular prism with 8 cubes in each layer. The prism had 4 layers. What is the volume of the rectangular prisms?

_____

Test Prep

7. Which is the volume of this figure?

   A. 15 cubic units   **B.** 20 cubic units

   C. 30 cubic units   **D.** 35 cubic units

8. **Writing in Math** Explain how you found the volume of the figure in Exercise 7.

_____

Name_____

Writing to Describe

Polygons Use geometric terms to describe two ways the triangle and the trapezoid are alike.

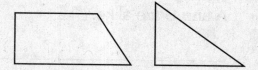

Tips for writing a good math description:

• Write down all the geometric terms that tell about the shapes in the group.

• Look for the geometric terms that tell how the shapes are alike.

• Use these geometric terms to tell about, or describe, how the shapes are alike.

Example:

Geometric terms that describe how the trapezoid and the triangle are alike:

     Right angles

     Polygons

     Not symmetric

The trapezoid and the triangle both are polygons. They both have a right angle. Neither of them is symmetric.

Write to describe.

1. Write statements that describe how the figures at the right are alike.

_____

_____

_____

2. Write statements that describe how the figures are different.

_____

_____

_____

PROBLEM-SOLVING SKILL
Writing to Describe

1. Write a statement to describe how
A and B are alike.

A

B

_____

_____

2. Write a statement describing how A and B are different.

_____

_____

3. How are the cone and the cylinder alike?

_____

_____

4. How are the cone and the cylinder different?

_____

_____

5. Tina turned a parallelogram as shown. How are
the two parallelograms alike? How are they different?

_____

_____

_____

6. **Reasoning** I am a solid figure. My faces are quadrilaterals.
Two faces are squares. What am I?

_____

PROBLEM-SOLVING APPLICATION
Kay's New Home

Kay's family has just moved into a new home. Here is a map that shows the house and the land it sits on.

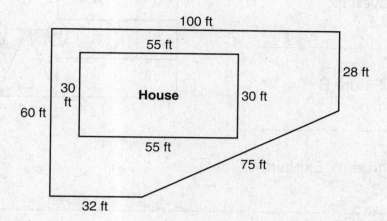

What is the perimeter of the land?

Remember, to find perimeter, add up all of the sides of the figure.

$$100 + 28 + 75 + 32 + 60 = 295 \text{ ft}$$

The land on which Kay's house sits has a perimeter of 295 ft.

---

1. What is the perimeter of Kay's house?

_____

2. Kay's father built a garden in the back yard. What is the area of the garden?

3.

Kay's mother set up a sandbox. What is the shape of the sandbox?

_____

Garden

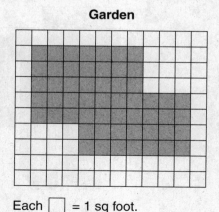

Each ☐ = 1 sq foot.

Name_____

PROBLEM-SOLVING APPLICATIONS
Polygons and Volume

Use the figure for Exercises 1–4.

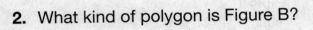

1. How many polygons are there in the figure?
   Do not count ones that overlap.

   _____

2. What kind of polygon is Figure B?

   _____

3. Are Figures H and I congruent? Explain.

   _____

   _____

   _____

4. Jeff says that Figures C and F have the same area. Do you
   agree? Explain.

   _____

   _____

   _____

5. Karen made a robot model out of cubes.
   What is the volume of the robot?

   _____

Name_____

Equal Parts of a Whole

A whole can be divided into equal parts in different ways.

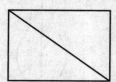
2 equal parts
halves

3 equal parts
thirds

4 equal parts
fourths

5 equal parts
fifths

6 equal parts
sixths

8 equal parts
eighths

10 equal parts
tenths

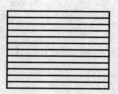
12 equal parts
twelfths

Tell if each shows equal parts or unequal parts.

1.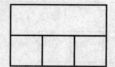

_____

2.

_____

3.

_____

Name the equal parts of the whole.

4.

_____

5.

6.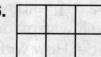

7. Using grid paper, draw a picture of a whole that is divided into thirds.

8. **Reasoning** How many equal parts are there when you divide a figure into fifths? _____

Name_____

Equal Parts of a Whole

Tell if each shows equal parts or unequal parts.

1.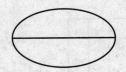

2.

3.

4.

_____   _____   _____   _____

Name the equal parts of the whole.

5.

6.

7.

_____   _____   _____

8.

9.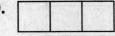

10.

_____   _____   _____

11. Amanda's grandmother made a quilt for Amanda's bed.
    The quilt was made of 9 squares. Each square was
    2 ft wide. How wide was Amanda's quilt?

Test Prep

12. Which is the name of 12 equal parts of a whole?

    A. Sixths   **B.** Twelfths   **C.** Halves   **D.** Tenths

13. **Writing in Math** Amanda says her quilt has 9 equal parts. Jeremy
    says it has 3 equal parts. Can they both be correct? Explain.

_____

Name_____

Naming Fractional Parts

You can write a fraction to describe the equal parts of a whole. The bottom part of the fraction is called the **denominator**. It tells how many equal parts the whole is divided into.

There are 5 equal parts. One is shaded.

$\frac{1}{5}$ ← Numerator
← Denominator

The top part of the fraction is called the **numerator**. It tells how many of the equal parts of the whole are specified.

$\frac{2}{3}$ of the circle is shaded.

$\frac{1}{2}$ of the square is shaded.

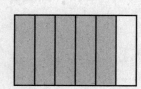

$\frac{5}{6}$ of the rectangle is shaded.

Write the fraction of each figure that is shaded.

1.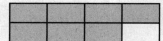

2.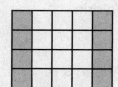

3.

_____   _____   _____

Draw a figure to show each fraction.

4. $\frac{1}{3}$ **5.** $\frac{5}{12}$

6. Reasoning A shape is $\frac{1}{7}$ shaded. How many parts are not shaded?

_____

Name_____

Naming Fractional Parts

Write the fraction of each figure that is shaded.

1.

2.

3.

4.

_____   _____   _____

Draw a picture to show each fraction.

5. $\frac{1}{3}$ 6. three eighths   7. one fourth

Valerie and Austin went bowling. They tried to knock down 10 pins with a bowling ball. Valerie knocked down 7 pins on her first turn. Austin knocked down 4 pins on his turn. Use this information for Exercises 8–11.

8. What fraction of the pins did Valerie knock down?   _____

9. **Reasoning** What fraction of Austin's pins were still standing after his turn?   _____

Test Prep

10. Which fraction shows the number of pins still standing after Valerie's turn?

    A. $\frac{9}{10}$ B. $\frac{7}{10}$ C. $\frac{5}{10}$ D. $\frac{3}{10}$

11. **Writing in Math** Clare decided to bowl after Austin. She knocked down 5 pins. Explain how you can find what fraction of the pins are still standing.

_____

_____

_____

Name _____

Equivalent Fractions

Figure A has 1 out of 2 parts shaded.
The fraction which is shaded is $\frac{1}{2}$.

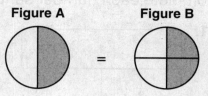

Figure A   =   Figure B

Figure B has 2 out of 4 parts shaded.
The fraction which is shaded is $\frac{2}{4}$.

Both figures have the same amount shaded. This means that the fractions $\frac{1}{2}$ and $\frac{2}{4}$ are equivalent. They both state that half of the figure is shaded.

So, $\frac{2}{4} = \frac{1}{2}$.

Complete each number sentence.

1.

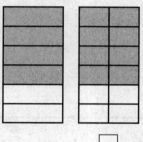

$$\frac{4}{6} = \frac{\boxed{}}{12}$$

2.

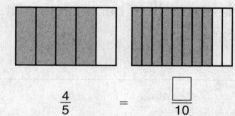

$$\frac{4}{5} = \frac{\boxed{}}{10}$$

Continue each pattern.

3.

$$\frac{1}{3} = \frac{2}{6} = \frac{\boxed{}}{9} = \frac{4}{\boxed{}}$$

4.

$$\frac{1}{5} = \frac{2}{10} = \frac{\boxed{}}{15} = \frac{4}{\boxed{}} = \frac{\boxed{}}{\boxed{}}$$

5. Reasoning Mary and Bill are each reading the same book. Mary read $\frac{1}{4}$ of the book. Bill says that since he read $\frac{2}{8}$ of the book, he read more. Is Bill correct? Explain.

_____

_____

_____

Name_____

Equivalent Fractions

Complete each number sentence.

1.
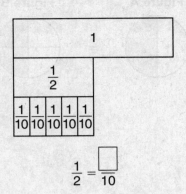

$$\frac{1}{2} = \frac{\boxed{}}{10}$$

2.
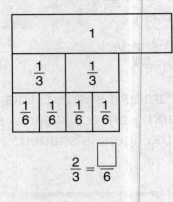

$$\frac{2}{3} = \frac{\boxed{}}{6}$$

3.
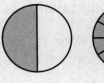

$$\frac{1}{2} = \frac{\boxed{}}{12}$$

4. Reasoning Samuel has read $\frac{5}{6}$ of his assignment. Judy has read $\frac{10}{12}$ of her assignment. Who has read more? Explain.

_____

_____

5. One half of the square is shaded. Draw three more ways to show $\frac{1}{2}$.

Test Prep

6. Which completes the pattern? $\frac{2}{3} = \frac{4}{6} = \frac{6}{9} = \frac{8}{12} = \frac{10}{\blacksquare}$

A. 4   **B.** 8   **C.** 12   **D.** 15

7. Writing in Math Amy finished $\frac{6}{12}$ of the problems on her timed test. Jackson finished $\frac{4}{6}$ of the problems on the timed test. Did they finish the same fraction of the problems? Explain.

_____

_____

Name_____

Comparing and Ordering Fractions

Compare $\frac{1}{3}$ and $\frac{4}{8}$.

Figure A   **Figure B**

$\frac{1}{3}$ $\frac{4}{8}$

Both figures are the same size. One has been divided into thirds, and the other has been divided into eighths. You can see that more of Figure B, $\frac{4}{8}$, is shaded than Figure A, $\frac{1}{3}$. So $\frac{4}{8}$ is greater than $\frac{1}{3}$.

$\frac{4}{8} > \frac{1}{3}$

Order $\frac{1}{4}$, $\frac{1}{3}$, and $\frac{3}{4}$ from greatest to least.

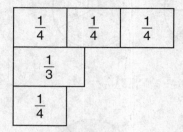

$\frac{3}{4} > \frac{1}{3}$

$\frac{1}{3} > \frac{1}{4}$

So, the fractions in order from greatest to least are $\frac{3}{4}$, $\frac{1}{3}$, $\frac{1}{4}$.

Compare. Write $>$, $<$, or $=$.

1.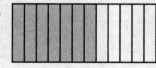

$\frac{1}{5}$ _____ $\frac{2}{6}$

2.

$\frac{6}{8}$ _____ $\frac{3}{4}$

3.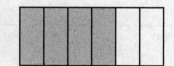

$\frac{7}{12}$ _____ $\frac{4}{6}$

4. Order $\frac{1}{5}$, $\frac{1}{2}$, and $\frac{3}{10}$ from greatest to least.

_____

$\frac{1}{10}$	$\frac{1}{10}$	$\frac{1}{10}$	$\frac{1}{10}$	$\frac{1}{10}$	$\frac{1}{10}$	$\frac{1}{10}$
$\frac{1}{5}$	$\frac{1}{5}$	$\frac{1}{5}$	$\frac{1}{5}$
	$\frac{1}{2}$

Name_____

Comparing and Ordering Fractions

Compare. Write >, <, or =.

1.

$\frac{1}{8}$ ◯ $\frac{1}{6}$

2.

$\frac{1}{2}$ ◯ $\frac{2}{3}$

3.

$\frac{7}{8}$ ◯ $\frac{9}{12}$

4.

$\frac{1}{8}$	$\frac{1}{8}$	$\frac{1}{8}$	$\frac{1}{8}$	$\frac{1}{8}$	$\frac{1}{8}$

$\frac{1}{4}$	$\frac{1}{4}$	$\frac{1}{4}$

$\frac{6}{8}$ ◯ $\frac{3}{4}$

Order from least to greatest.

5. $\frac{5}{10}$ $\frac{1}{3}$ $\frac{6}{8}$

$\frac{1}{8}$	$\frac{1}{8}$	$\frac{1}{8}$	$\frac{1}{8}$	$\frac{1}{8}$	$\frac{1}{8}$

$\frac{1}{10}$	$\frac{1}{10}$	$\frac{1}{10}$	$\frac{1}{10}$	$\frac{1}{10}$

$\frac{1}{3}$

_____

6. $\frac{7}{10}$ of your body is made of water. Is more than $\frac{1}{2}$ of your body water? Explain.

_____

_____

Test Prep

7. Which fraction is equal to $\frac{1}{5}$?

   A. $\frac{2}{10}$ **B.** $\frac{3}{10}$ **C.** $\frac{1}{15}$ **D.** $\frac{2}{15}$

8. **Writing in Math** Explain why $\frac{1}{8}$ is greater than $\frac{1}{10}$, but less than $\frac{1}{3}$.

_____

_____

Name_____

Estimating Fractional Amounts

You can estimate a fractional amount by comparing the amount to fractions you know.

Estimate the fraction of the wall that is painted black.

About $\frac{3}{4}$ of the wall is painted black.

Estimate the fraction of the pie that is left.

About $\frac{1}{2}$ of the pie is left.

Estimate the amount that is shaded.

1.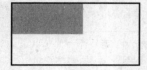

_____

2.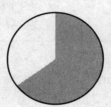

_____

3.

_____

4.

_____

5.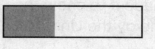

_____

6.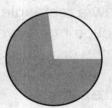

_____

7. Number Sense About how much of the casserole is left over?

_____

Name_____

Estimating Fractional Amounts

Estimate the amount that is left.

1.

2.

3.

_____   _____   _____

Estimate the amount that is shaded.

4.

5.

6.

_____   _____   _____

7. **Reasoning** About what fraction of the circle in
   Exercise 6 is not shaded?

_____

The United States produces about $\frac{1}{5}$ of the world's energy, but it
uses about $\frac{1}{4}$ of the world's energy.

8. Draw a rectangle and shade it to show the
   fraction of the world's energy the United
   States produces.

Test Prep

9. About how much is shaded?

   A. $\frac{1}{5}$ **B.** $\frac{1}{8}$

   C. $\frac{1}{3}$ **D.** $\frac{2}{3}$

10. **Writing in Math** Draw a rectangle and shade
    about three-fourths of it. Write a fraction for the
    shaded and the unshaded parts.

_____

Fractions on the Number Line

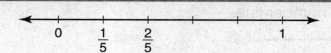

Here is the number line for a denominator of 5, or fifths.

The next two fractions would be $\frac{3}{5}$ and $\frac{4}{5}$.

Write the missing fractions for each number line.

1.

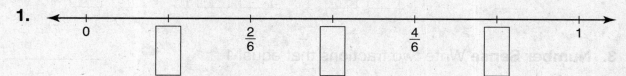

2.

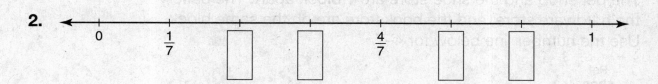

3.

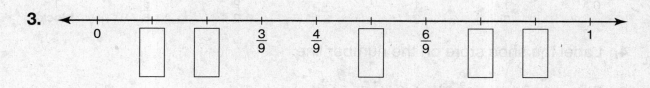

4.

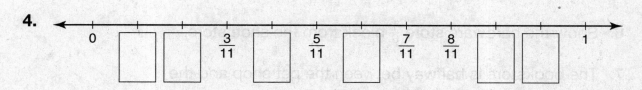

5. Number Sense What fraction would come after $\frac{5}{8}$ on a number line divided into eighths? _____

Fractions on the Number Line

Write the missing fractions for each number line.

1.

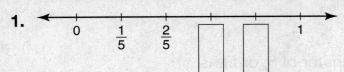

2.

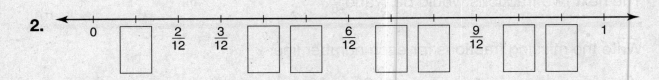

3. Number Sense Write two fractions that equal 1.   _____

The pet shop and the shoe store are 1 block apart. The bakery, the hardware store, and the bookstore are on the same block. Use the number line below for 4–7.

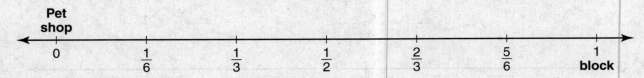

4. Label the shoe store on the number line.

5. Show the bakery $\frac{2}{6}$ block from the pet shop.

6. Show the hardware store $\frac{1}{6}$ block from the shoe store.

7. The bookstore is halfway between the pet shop and the shoe store. Label it.

Test Prep

8. Which fraction is equal to 1?

A. $\frac{3}{3}$ **B.** $\frac{7}{8}$ **C.** $\frac{9}{12}$ **D.** $\frac{11}{12}$

9. Writing in Math How can you use a number line to order $\frac{2}{8}$, $\frac{7}{8}$, $\frac{3}{8}$, and $\frac{5}{8}$ from greatest to least?

_____

_____

Name_____

Fractions and Sets

When a group of individual items is collected into a whole, you can use a fraction to name a part of the group.

What fraction of the marbles are black?

 $\dfrac{3}{8}$ ← Number of black marbles
← Total number of marbles

$\dfrac{3}{8}$ of the marbles are black.

---

1. What fraction of the toys are balls? _____

2. What fraction of the fruits are oranges? _____

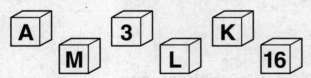

3. What fraction of the blocks have letters on them? _____

4. What fraction of the days of the week begin with the letter *T*? _____

Draw a picture to show each fraction of a set.

5. $\dfrac{3}{5}$ of the squares are shaded.

6. $\dfrac{2}{3}$ of the balls are footballs.

7. Reasoning Out of 6 cats, 2 are tan colored. What fraction of cats are not tan? _____

Fractions and Sets

1. What fraction of the
   plants are flowers? _____

2. What fraction of the
   boats are sailboats? _____

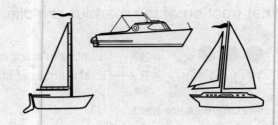

3. What fraction of the utensils are forks?

_____

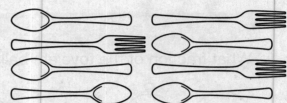

Draw a picture to show the fraction of a set.

4. $\frac{3}{5}$ of the shapes are circles.

5. **Reasoning** Fran cut her sandwich into 6 pieces.
   If Fran ate $\frac{1}{3}$ of her sandwich, how many pieces
   did she eat? _____

Test Prep

6. Pamela has 4 pink hair ribbons, 3 green hair ribbons, and
   2 blue hair ribbons. What fraction of Pamela's hair ribbons
   are green?

   A. $\frac{4}{5}$ **B.** $\frac{3}{4}$ **C.** $\frac{3}{6}$ **D.** $\frac{3}{9}$

7. **Writing in Math** Write a problem about 12 eggs. Make the
   answer to your problem a fraction.

   _____

   _____

   _____

Name_____

Finding Fractional Parts of a Set

How to divide to find a fraction of a set:

Find $\frac{1}{3}$ of 15 triangles.

First, divide the 15 triangles into 3 equal groups.

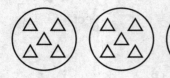

$15 \div 3 = 5$

So, $\frac{1}{3}$ of 15 = 5.

Find $\frac{1}{3}$ of 12 squares.

First, divide the 12 squares into 3 equal groups.

$12 \div 3 = 4$

So, $\frac{1}{3}$ of 12 = 4.

---

1. Find $\frac{1}{2}$ of 10 blocks.

$10 \div 2 =$ _____

$\frac{1}{2}$ of 10 = _____

2. Find $\frac{1}{6}$ of 18 triangles.

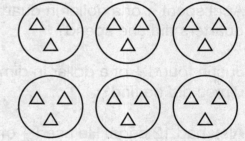

$18 \div 6 =$ _____

$\frac{1}{6}$ of 18 = _____

3. $\frac{1}{3}$ of 9 = _____

4. $\frac{1}{2}$ of 24 = _____

5. $\frac{1}{5}$ of 25 = _____

6. $\frac{1}{4}$ of 40 = _____

7. Number Sense When you divide 50 by 2, what fraction of 50 are you finding? Find the answer.

_____

Name_____

Finding Fractional Parts of a Set

1. Find $\frac{1}{3}$ of 9 books.

2. Find $\frac{1}{6}$ of 12 pencils.

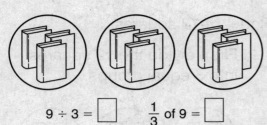

$9 \div 3 = \square$ $\frac{1}{3}$ of $9 = \square$

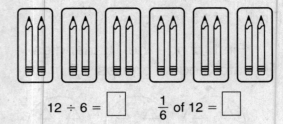

$12 \div 6 = \square$ $\frac{1}{6}$ of $12 = \square$

3. Find $\frac{1}{5}$ of 10. _____

4. Find $\frac{1}{2}$ of 18. _____

5. Find $\frac{1}{3}$ of 21. _____

6. Find $\frac{1}{4}$ of 20. _____

7. Number Sense To find $\frac{1}{3}$ of 24, what two numbers should you divide?

_____

8. April spent $\frac{1}{2}$ of a dollar in quarters. How many quarters did she spend?

_____

9. Justin found $\frac{1}{5}$ of a dollar in dimes. How many dimes did he find?

_____

10. Alex had 12 eggs. He used $\frac{1}{4}$ of them in an omelet. How many eggs did he use?

_____

11. Hannah used $\frac{1}{3}$ yd of ribbon to wrap a package. How many inches did she use? (Hint: There are 36 in. in 1 yd.)

_____

Test Prep

12. Which is $\frac{1}{8}$ of 64?

A. 8   **B.** 10   **C.** 12   **D.** 14

13. Writing in Math Draw a picture to show $\frac{1}{5}$ of 25.

Name_____

Adding and Subtracting Fractions

R 9-9

Adding fractions:

Find $\frac{2}{4} + \frac{1}{4}$.

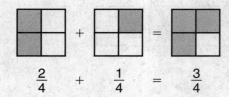

$$\frac{2}{4} \quad + \quad \frac{1}{4} \quad = \quad \frac{3}{4}$$

Add the numerators but keep the denominators the same.

So, $\frac{2}{4} + \frac{1}{4} = \frac{3}{4}$.

Subtracting fractions:

Find $\frac{5}{6} - \frac{4}{6}$.

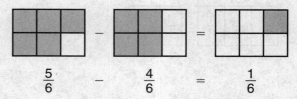

$$\frac{5}{6} \quad - \quad \frac{4}{6} \quad = \quad \frac{1}{6}$$

You subtract the numerators, and the denominator remains the same.

So, $\frac{5}{6} - \frac{4}{6} = \frac{1}{6}$.

Add or subtract. You may use fraction strips or draw a picture to help.

1. $\frac{1}{3} + \frac{1}{3} =$ _____

2. $\frac{3}{5} - \frac{2}{5} =$ _____

3. $\frac{4}{8} + \frac{1}{8} =$ _____

4. $\frac{5}{6} - \frac{2}{6} =$ _____

5. $\frac{10}{12} - \frac{5}{12} =$ _____

6. $\frac{4}{5} - \frac{1}{5} =$ _____

7. Reasoning Judy left $\frac{4}{5}$ of a pot of stew for Dan. Dan ate $\frac{2}{5}$ of what she left. What fraction of the pot of stew was left after Dan ate?

_____

© Pearson Education, Inc. 3

Name_____

Adding and Subtracting Fractions

Add or subtract. You may use fraction strips or draw a picture to help.

1. $\frac{3}{8} + \frac{2}{8} =$ _____

| $\frac{1}{8}$ | $\frac{1}{8}$ | $\frac{1}{8}$ | | $\frac{1}{8}$ | $\frac{1}{8}$ |

2. $\frac{7}{12} - \frac{5}{12} =$ _____

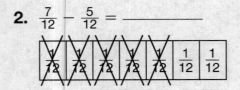

3. $\frac{6}{8} - \frac{3}{8} =$ _____

4. $\frac{4}{6} + \frac{1}{6} =$ _____

5. $\frac{11}{12} + \frac{1}{12} =$ _____

6. $\frac{3}{4} - \frac{1}{4} =$ _____

7. Jason's family ate $\frac{1}{3}$ of a watermelon one evening and $\frac{1}{3}$ of the watermelon another evening. What fraction of the watermelon did Jason's family eat altogether?

_____

8. Austin can weed $\frac{1}{5}$ of the garden in 1 hr. His mother can weed $\frac{2}{5}$ of the garden in 1 hr. What fraction of the garden can Austin and his mother weed together in 1 hr?

_____

9. Patricia is responsible for washing $\frac{6}{8}$ of the desks in her classroom. She has already washed $\frac{4}{8}$ of the desks. What fraction of the desks does she have left to wash?

_____

Test Prep

10. Which is the difference of $\frac{5}{8} - \frac{3}{8}$?

A. $\frac{8}{8}$ B. $\frac{8}{16}$ C. $\frac{2}{8}$ D. $\frac{2}{16}$

11. **Writing in Math** Write an addition problem with $\frac{3}{5}$ as the sum.

_____

_____

_____

_____

Name_____

Mixed Numbers

A mixed number is a combination of a whole number and a fraction. $5\frac{1}{2}$ is a mixed number. 5 is the whole number, and $\frac{1}{2}$ is the fraction.

How many circles are shown?

There are 2 whole circles and $\frac{1}{2}$ of another circle.

There are $2\frac{1}{2}$ circles shown.

The mixed number is $2\frac{1}{2}$.

How many squares are shown?

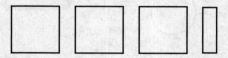

There are 3 whole squares and $\frac{1}{4}$ of another square.

There are $3\frac{1}{4}$ squares shown.

The mixed number is $3\frac{1}{4}$.

Write a mixed number for each picture.

1.

2.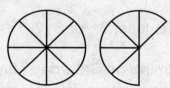

3.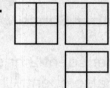

_____   _____   _____

Draw a picture to show each mixed number.

4. $3\frac{2}{5}$

5. $2\frac{1}{3}$

6. **Reasoning** There are 12 doughnuts in a dozen. How many are there in $2\frac{1}{2}$ dozen?

_____

Mixed Numbers

Write a mixed number for each picture.

1.

2.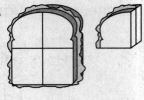

3.

_____   _____   _____

Draw a picture to show each number.

4. $2\frac{3}{4}$

5. $1\frac{2}{3}$

6. **Number Sense** Which is less, $3\frac{2}{3}$ or $3\frac{3}{4}$?   _____

7. Esther spent 2 hr swimming on Saturday afternoon. She also spent $\frac{1}{2}$ hr writing letters. Write a mixed number to show the total time Esther spent swimming and writing letters.   _____

8. The black rhinoceros lives an average of 15 years. How many decades does the rhinoceros live? Write your answer as a mixed number. (Hint: There are 10 years in a decade.)   _____

Test Prep

9. Which mixed number is greatest?

   A. $1\frac{1}{2}$ **B.** $1\frac{1}{3}$ **C.** $1\frac{1}{4}$ **D.** $1\frac{2}{3}$

10. **Writing in Math** Tom said that 15 months is more than $1\frac{1}{2}$ years. Is he right? Explain.

_____

PROBLEM-SOLVING STRATEGY

Solve a Simpler Problem

Weeks How many weeks are there in $4\frac{1}{2}$ years? Remember, there are 52 weeks in a year.

Read and Understand

Step 1: What do you know?

There are 52 weeks in a year.

Step 2: What are you trying to find?

The number of weeks in $4\frac{1}{2}$ years

Plan and Solve

Step 3: What strategy will you use?   **Strategy:** Solve a simpler problem

Simpler Problem No. 1: How many weeks are there in 4 years?

I know there are 52 weeks in one year. So to find the number of weeks in 4 years, I can multiply 52 × 4, or add 52 + 52 + 52 + 52. There are 208 weeks in 4 years.

Simpler Problem No. 2: How many weeks are there in $\frac{1}{2}$ of a year?

I learned that to find a fraction of a number, I divide the number by the denominator of the fraction. 52 divided by 2 is 26. There are 26 weeks in $\frac{1}{2}$ of a year.

Solve the problem.

To solve the problem, I need to add the 4 years of weeks to the $\frac{1}{2}$ year of weeks. 208 + 26 = 234. So, there are 234 weeks in $4\frac{1}{2}$ years.

Look Back and Check

Step 4: Is your work correct?

Yes. I know that there are close to 50 weeks in a year, and so in 4 years there are close to 200 weeks, and in 5 years there are close to 250 weeks. 234 weeks is close to halfway between 200 and 250.

---

1. Cindy has a pad with 50 pieces of paper in it. Last week she used $\frac{1}{5}$ of the paper. This week she gave 12 sheets of the paper to a friend. How many sheets of paper does Cindy have left?

   _____

Name_____

Solve a Simpler Problem

Solve. Write the answer in a complete sentence.

1. If a deer can travel 12 mi per hour, how far can a deer travel in 15 minutes?

   a. How far can a deer travel in 1 hour?

   _____

   b. How many 15 min periods are in 1 hour?

   _____

   c. How can you find the distance a deer can travel in 15 minutes? Solve the problem.

   _____

2. How many diamonds are in the figure?

   _____

   _____

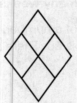

3. Hector's family began their vacation on July 3. First, they drove for 2 days. Then they stayed with relatives for 3 days. After visiting relatives, they drove a whole day to get to the ocean. They vacationed at the ocean for 5 days. It took them 3 days to drive back home. How many weeks was Hector's family gone?

   _____

4. Maria bought 13 comic books at a garage sale. She kept 4 comic books and divided the rest equally between some friends. Each friend got 3 comic books. With how many friends did Maria share the comic books?

   _____

To use a ruler, line up the object with the 0 mark.

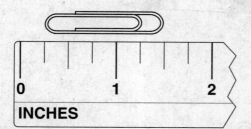

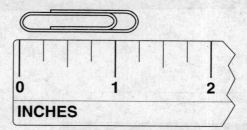

Wrong way. The paper clip is not lined up with the zero.

Right way. By lining the paper clip up with the zero, you can see that it is $1\frac{1}{4}$ inches long, that is 1 inch long to the nearest inch.

Estimate each length. Then measure it to the nearest inch.

1.

_____

2.

_____

3.

_____

4. GLUE STICK

_____

5. Number Sense Estimate the length of one of your index fingers. Then measure. Record the measurement to the nearest inch.

_____

Length

Estimate each length. Then measure to the nearest inch.

1.

_____

2.

_____

3.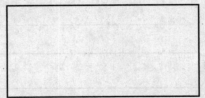

_____

4. Measure the perimeter of the rectangle to the nearest inch.

_____

Test Prep

5. Measure the line segment to the nearest inch.

   A. 2 in.   **B.** 3 in.   **C.** 4 in.   **D.** 5 in.

6. **Writing in Math** Explain how to use a ruler to measure to the nearest inch.

_____

_____

_____

_____

Name_____

Measuring to the Nearest $\frac{1}{2}$ and $\frac{1}{4}$ Inch

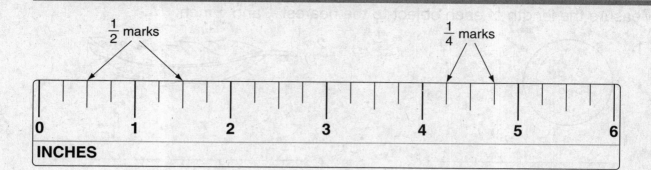

$\frac{1}{2}$ marks

$\frac{1}{4}$ marks

How long is the peanut to the nearest $\frac{1}{2}$ inch?

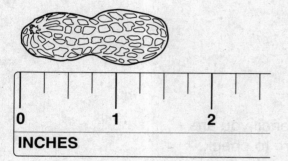

The peanut is $1\frac{1}{2}$ in. to the nearest $\frac{1}{2}$ inch.

How long is the chalk to the nearest $\frac{1}{4}$ inch?

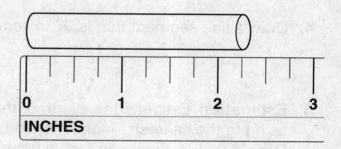

The chalk is $2\frac{1}{4}$ in. to the nearest $\frac{1}{4}$ inch.

Measure the length of each object to the nearest $\frac{1}{2}$ and $\frac{1}{4}$ inch.

1.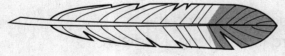

_____

2.

_____

3.

_____

4.

_____

Name_____

Measuring to the Nearest $\frac{1}{2}$ and $\frac{1}{4}$ Inch

Measure the length of each object to the nearest $\frac{1}{2}$ and $\frac{1}{4}$ inch.

1.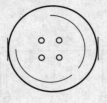

_____

2.

_____

3. ├─────────────────────────────────┤

_____

4. Draw a line segment that is $3\frac{3}{4}$ in. long.

5. **Estimation** Estimate the length of the pencil you are using to the nearest $\frac{1}{4}$ inch. Then measure to check. Record your estimate and measurement.

_____

Test Prep

6. Which can NOT be a length to the nearest $\frac{1}{4}$ inch?

   A. $\frac{1}{4}$ in. **B.** $\frac{1}{2}$ in. **C.** $\frac{3}{8}$ in. **D.** 1 in.

7. **Writing in Math** Eric and Madison both measured the same trading card. Eric says the card is 3 in. long. Madison says it is $2\frac{3}{4}$ in. long. Their teacher says they are both correct. How is this possible?

_____

_____

_____

_____

Length in Feet and Inches

Longer lengths can be measured in feet. 1 ft is 12 in. long.

To change a measurement from feet into inches, you can multiply the number of feet by 12.

2 ft = _____ in.?

2 × 12 = 24

So, 2 ft = 24 in.

How many inches are in 4 ft, 2 in.?

First multiply.

4 × 12 in. = 48 in.

Then add the extra inches.

48 in. + 2 in. = 50 in.

So, 4 ft, 2 in. = 50 in.

Write each measurement in inches. You may make a table to help.

1. 1 foot, 3 inches

_____

2. 5 feet, 6 inches

_____

3. 2 feet

_____

4. 3 feet, 2 inches

_____

5. 1 foot, 9 inches

_____

6. 6 feet, 3 inches

_____

7. 8 feet

_____

8. 4 feet, 8 inches

_____

9. 7 feet, 7 inches

_____

10. Number Sense Marsha broad jumped 5 ft, 1 in.
How many inches did she jump? _____

Name_____

Length in Feet and Inches

Write each measurement in inches. You may make a table to help.

1. 3 ft, 3 in. _____

2. 1 ft, 9 in. _____

3. 2 ft, 7 in. _____

4. 5 ft, 6 in. _____

5. 4 ft, 8 in. _____

6. 1 ft, 11 in. _____

7. Finish the table to find how many inches are in 7 ft, 8 in. Write the answer in a complete sentence.

Feet	1	2	3	4	5	6	7
Inches							

_____

African elephant	13 ft tall
Whale shark	41 ft 6 in. long
Stick insect	1 ft 3 in. long
Giraffe	19 ft tall

8. How many inches long is the stick insect? _____

9. How many inches taller is a giraffe than an African elephant? _____

10. List the animals in order from largest to smallest.

_____

_____

Test Prep

11. Which measurement is equal to 3 ft, 7 in.?

A. 37 in.　　　**B.** 43 in.　　　**C.** 44 in.　　　**D.** 73 in.

12. **Writing in Math** Name something you would not measure in feet and inches. Tell why.

_____

_____

Feet, Yards, and Miles

Customary Units of Length

12 in. = 1 ft

3 ft = 1 yd

36 in. = 1 yd

5,280 ft = 1 mi

1,760 yd = 1 mi

How do you change units?

How many inches are in 4 yd?

Make a table.

Yards	1	2	3	4
Inches	36	72	108	144

There are 144 in. in 4 yd.

How many feet are in 6 yd?

Remember: 1 yd = 3 ft

Multiply.

6×3 ft = 18 ft

There are 18 ft in 6 yd.

Change the units. You may make a table to help.

1. How many feet are in 3 yd?

_____

2. How many inches are in 3 yd?

_____

3. How many feet are in 7 yd?

_____

4. How many feet are in 11 yd?

_____

Compare. Write $<$, $>$, or $=$.

5. 27 in. $\bigcirc$ 2 ft

6. 1 mi $\bigcirc$ 2,000 yd

7. 4 yd $\bigcirc$ 12 in.

8. 72 in. $\bigcirc$ 2 yd

Choose the better estimate.

9. A sleeping bag: 7 ft or 7 yd _____

Name_____

Feet, Yards, and Miles

Change the units. You may make a table to help.

1. How many feet are in 7 yd?

_____

2. How many inches are in 2 yd?

_____

3. How many feet are in 5 yd?

_____

4. How many inches are in 3 yd?

_____

Compare. Write <, >, or =.

5. 90 in. ◯ 3 yd

6. 1,800 yd ◯ 1 mi

Circle the better estimate.

7. The depth of a swimming pool

10 ft or 10 mi

8. The length of your desk

2 ft or 2 yd

9. A baseball diamond has 90 ft between each base.
A softball diamond has 60 ft between each base.
How many yards longer is the space between
bases on a baseball diamond than a softball
diamond?

_____

Test Prep

10. Which unit would be best to measure the distance around
the equator?

A. Inches   **B.** Feet   **C.** Yards   **D.** Miles

11. Writing in Math Explain how to use multiplication to
convert yards to feet.

_____

_____

_____

Name_____

Extra or Missing Information

Helmets Henry is working to buy a new bike helmet. The helmet costs $22. Henry makes $5 an hour helping his mother plant flowers. How much has he made so far?

Read and Understand

Step 1: Tell what the question is asking.

How much money has Henry earned so far?

Step 2: Identify key facts and details.

Henry earns $5 per hour. The helmet costs $22.

Plan and Solve

Step 3: Find the extra or missing information.

I do not need to know how much the helmet costs. I do need to know how many hours Henry has worked so far. The problem cannot be solved without knowing the number of hours.

Decide if each problem has extra information or missing information. Solve if you have enough information.

1. There are 3 tables that will be used to serve food at a banquet. The tables are each 6 ft, 2 in. long. How many inches long are the tables if they are put end to end?

   _____

2. Which of the three children lost a tooth first?

   _____

   _____

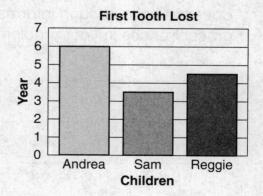

First Tooth Lost

3. How old was Reggie when he lost his last baby tooth?

   _____

© Pearson Education, Inc. 3

Extra or Missing Information

Decide if each problem has extra information or missing information. Solve if you have enough information.

1. Mrs. James wants to purchase new carpet for her bedroom. The carpet costs $13 per foot. Her bedroom is 5 ft shorter than the living room. How much carpet will she need?

_____

2. For each time Kendra walks Mr. Karl's dog, he gives her $3. Kendra walks the dog for 30 min each time. If she walks the dog on Monday, Tuesday, and Thursday, how much money does Kendra make each week for walking Mr. Karl's dog?

_____

_____

3. Dylan trades baseball cards with his friends. He received most of his baseball cards as a gift from his grandmother. If Dylan trades 58 baseball cards away and gets 62 back, how many more cards does he have now?

_____

_____

4. **Writing in Math** Write a story problem that does not have enough information. Use the grocery prices in your problem.

Groceries	
Bread	$2.29
Milk	$3.09
Cheese	$1.50
Orange juice	$3.25
Cereal	$4.79

_____

_____

_____

Name_____

The Family Reunion

The Angelo family had a reunion. Over 200 family members from all over the country attended.

Donna Angelo made special pies for the family members to eat. One pie was equally divided into 5 pieces. Bill Angelo ate $\frac{2}{5}$ of the pie. How many pieces were left?

Remember to subtract fractions with the same denominators. First, subtract the numerators. Leave the denominators the same.

$$\frac{5}{5} - \frac{2}{5} = \frac{3}{5}$$

So, 3 pieces of pie were left.

1. Diana Angelo is 36 years old. Her son Ted is $\frac{1}{4}$ of her age. How old is Ted?

   _____

2. When George Angelo was born he was 16 in. tall. When he was 10, he was 4 ft, 10 in. tall. As an adult George is 6 ft, 2 in. tall. How many inches did George grow from when he was born until he became an adult? Give your answer in inches.

   _____

3. Heidi Angelo is making a friendship bracelet for her cousin Mara. She has 3 beads on the bracelet. Two of the beads are $\frac{3}{8}$ in. wide. The other bead is $\frac{1}{8}$ in. wide. How much room will the beads take up altogether on her bracelet?

   _____

4. The family ate two kinds of submarine sandwiches. The turkey sub was 4 ft, 2 in. long. The beef sub was 53 in. long. Which sub was longer?

   _____

Name_____

Food Servings

The table shows an example of one serving of each of the food groups in the food pyramid.

Group	Example of 1 Serving
Milk, yogurt, and cheese	$1\frac{1}{2}$ oz of cheese
Meat, beans, eggs, and nuts	$\frac{2}{3}$ c of nuts
Vegetables	$\frac{3}{4}$ c vegetable juice
Fruit	1 medium apple
Bread, cereal, and pasta	1 slice of bread

Solve. Write your answer in a complete sentence.

1. Patsy and Kyle each drank 1 serving of carrot juice. How many cups of carrot juice did they drink altogether?

   _____

   _____

2. Alex has $\frac{4}{5}$ c of walnuts. Does he have enough for 1 serving? Explain.

   _____

   _____

3. Luke has $1\frac{3}{6}$ oz of cheese. He says that is enough for one serving. Do you agree? Explain.

   _____

   _____

4. A loaf of bread will provide 1 serving each for Julia and her brother for 5 days. How many slices of bread are in the loaf?

   _____

Name_____

Tenths

Tenths show 10 equal parts of a whole. Fractions and decimals can be used to write tenths.

Fractions and decimals:

Word form: one tenth
Fraction: $\frac{1}{10}$
Decimal: 0.1

Mixed numbers and decimals:

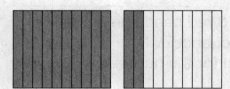

Word form: one and six tenths
Fraction: $1\frac{6}{10}$
Decimal: 1.6

Write a fraction and a decimal for each shaded part.

1.  _____

2.  _____

3. 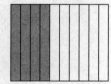 _____

Write each as a decimal.

4. $\frac{3}{10}$ _____

5. $1\frac{5}{10}$ _____

6. $4\frac{6}{10}$ _____

7. one and three tenths _____

8. six and one tenth _____

9. eight tenths _____

10. nine and nine tenths _____

11. Number Sense In the United States, $\frac{6}{10}$ of all potato products come from Idaho. Write the decimal to show how many U.S. potato products come from Idaho. _____

Name_____

Tenths

Write a fraction and a decimal for each shaded part.

1.

2.

3.

_____ _____

Write each as a decimal.

4. $\frac{4}{10}$ _____   **5.** $7\frac{9}{10}$ _____

6. four and six tenths _____   **7.** eight tenths _____

8. Number Sense How many tenths are in 3.2? _____

9. It takes $8\frac{5}{10}$ min for light to get from the Sun to Earth. Write a decimal to show how long it takes. _____

10. Sylvia has 10 beads with different shapes: 3 red beads are heart shaped, 2 blue beads are star shaped, and 5 white beads are cylinder shaped. Write a decimal for the number of red heart-shaped beads.

_____

Test Prep

11. How many tenths are in 0.2?

A. 22   **B.** 20   **C.** 12   **D.** 2

12. Writing in Math Explain how to find the mixed number and decimal for nine and one tenth.

_____

_____

_____

Hundredths

Writing hundredths as fractions:

There are 100 squares.
Each square is one hundredth.
53 squares are shaded.
Word form: fifty-three hundredths
Fraction: $\frac{53}{100}$
Decimal: 0.53

Writing hundredths as mixed numbers:

In the left hand grid,
100 out of 100 squares
have been shaded. This
is one whole, or 1.
Word form: one and seventeen
hundredths
Fraction: $1\frac{17}{100}$
Decimal: 1.17

Write a fraction or mixed number and a decimal for each shaded part.

1.

_____

2.

_____

3.

_____

4.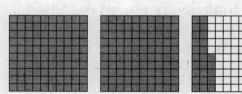

_____

Write each as a decimal.

5. $\frac{62}{100}$

_____

6. $1\frac{97}{100}$

_____

7. seven hundredths

_____

Name_____

Hundredths

Write a fraction or mixed number and a decimal for each shaded part.

1.

_____

2.

_____

3.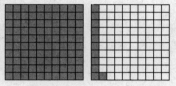

_____

4.

_____

Write each as a decimal.

5. $\frac{67}{100}$ _____

6. 91 hundredths _____

7. $4\frac{9}{100}$ _____

8. 48 hundredths _____

9. There are 100 players in Kim's soccer league. 15 of the players are on the Sharks. Write a fraction and a decimal to show what part of the players are on the Sharks.

_____

Test Prep

10. Which is the decimal for $\frac{82}{100}$?

A. 82   **B.** 8.2   **C.** 0.82   **D.** 0.082

11. Writing in Math Explain how to read the decimal 8.79.

_____

_____

_____

Name_____

Comparing and Ordering Decimals

You can use hundreds grids to compare decimals.

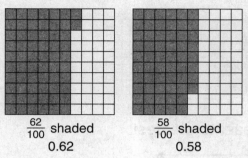

$\frac{62}{100}$ shaded
0.62

$\frac{58}{100}$ shaded
0.58

There are more squares shaded in 0.62 than in 0.58, so 0.62 is greater.
0.62 > 0.58

You can use number lines to order decimals.

Order 0.22, 0.13, and 0.37 from least to greatest.

Place the numbers on the number line. The number that is the farthest right is the greatest. The number that is the farthest left is the least.

0.13 < 0.22 < 0.37

So, the numbers in order from least to greatest are 0.13, 0.22, and 0.37.

Compare. Use <, >, or =.

1.

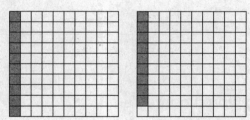

0.10 ◯ 0.09

Use the number line to order the numbers from least to greatest.

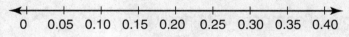

2. 0.22   0.27   0.19   _____

3. 0.04   0.40   0.21   _____

Name_____

Comparing and Ordering Decimals

Compare. Use <, >, or =.

1. 0.6 ◯ 0.60

2. 0.78 ◯ 0.68

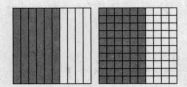

Use the number line to order the decimals from least to greatest.

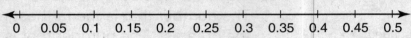

3. 0.15   0.5   0.25   _____

4. 0.47   0.35   0.4   _____

Order the decimals from least to greatest.

5. 0.34   0.42   0.36   _____

6. 0.07   0.7   0.71   _____

Test Prep

7. On a number line, which of the following would come between 0.12 and 0.2?

   A. 0.09   **B.** 0.18   **C.** 0.22   **D.** 0.91

8. Writing in Math Explain how to compare 0.34 and 0.27.

_____

_____

_____

_____

Name_____

Adding and Subtracting Decimals

You can use what you know about adding and subtracting whole numbers to add and subtract decimals. Just remember to line up the decimal points before adding or subtracting, and to place the decimal point in the answer.

Find 8.21 + 5.89.

Step 1	Step 2	Step 3	Step 4
Line up the decimal points.	Add the hundredths.	Add the tenths.	Add the ones. Write a decimal point in the sum.
8.21 + 5.89	1 8.21 + 5.89 0	1 1 8.21 + 5.89 10	1 1 8.21 + 5.89 14.10

Find 7.45 − 1.18.

Step 1	Step 2	Step 3	Step 4
Line up the decimal points.	Subtract the hundredths. Regroup if needed.	Subtract the tenths. Regroup if needed.	Subtract the ones. Write a decimal point in the difference.
7.45 − 1.18	3 15 7.45 − 1.18 7	3 15 7.45 − 1.18 27	3 15 7.45 − 1.18 6.27

Add.

1.	3.4 + 6.2	2.	0.47 + 1.61	3.	7.1 + 4.8	4.	2.50 + 1.23

Subtract.

5.	5.7 − 2.3	6.	7.92 − 5.18	7.	9.6 − 5.4	8.	1.56 − 1.02

9. Terry has $1.46 and Cindy has $1.64. How much money do they have altogether?

_____

Name_____

Adding and Subtracting Decimals

Add.

1. 0.9
    + 0.4

2. 3.47
    + 1.14

3. 3.1
    + 2.7

4. 4.72
    + 5.81

Subtract.

5. 5.2
    − 2.2

6. 9.51
    − 3.9

7. 3.8
    − 2.9

8. 8.78
    − 5.30

9. It is 3.41 mi from Kyle's house to the library. Michelle's house is 2.78 mi from the library. How much farther from the library is Kyle's house than Michelle's house?

_____

10. Sam bought a book at the bookstore for $6.97. Jasmine bought the same book for $3.74 on the Internet. How much more did Sam pay for the book than Jasmine?

_____

Test Prep

11. Which is the sum of 52.62 + 6.71?

    A. 45.91   **B.** 53.29   **C.** 59.33   **D.** 119.72

12. **Writing in Math** Without subtracting, tell which is greater, 2.3 − 1.7 or 1. Explain.

_____

_____

_____

PROBLEM-SOLVING STRATEGY

Make an Organized List

Posters Lisa has three posters that she would like to put on her door, but only two will fit, one above the other. One is green, one is red, and one is blue. How many different ways can she arrange the two posters on her door?

Read and Understand

Step 1: What do you know?

Two posters will fit on the door. Lisa has three posters. One poster will be above the other.

Step 2: What are you trying to find?

The number of ways two of the posters can be arranged on Lisa's door

Plan and Solve

Step 3: What strategy will you use?

Strategy: Make an organized list

B   B   R   R   G   G

R   G   B   G   B   R

There are 6 ways the posters can be arranged.

Look Back and Check

Step 4: Is your work correct?

Yes; there are no repeats, and all of the posters have been in the top position with each of the others, and the bottom position with each of the others.

Solve. Write the answer in a complete sentence.

1. Jenna, Mac, and Emily are having their picture taken for the yearbook. How many different ways can they line up in a straight line for the picture?

_____

_____

Name_____

Make an Organized List

Solve. Write the answer in a complete sentence.

1. How many ways can you arrange the letters A, B, C,
   and D? Continue the list to find all the ways.

A B C D	B A C D
A B D C	B A D C
A C B D	
A C D B	
A D B C	
A D C B	

   _____

   _____

2. Three marbles are in a jar: 1 red marble, 1 blue marble, and
   1 green marble. In how many different orders can you take
   the marbles out of the jar?

   _____

   _____

3. Beth's mother told her that she can choose 4 books from
   the book fair. There are 6 books that Beth would like to
   have. How many different combinations of 4 books could
   Beth choose from those 6?

   _____

   _____

4. Jim and Sarah are running for class president. Cayla and
   Daniel are running for vice president. How many
   combinations of students can be elected as class president
   and vice president?

   _____

   _____

Name _____

Centimeters and Decimeters

A centimeter (cm) is a unit of measurement that is used to measure small objects. A decimeter (dm) is 10 cm long.

1 dm = 10 cm

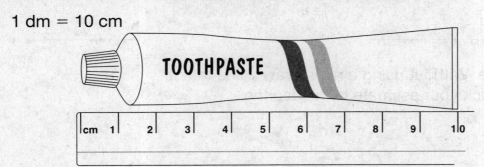

The tube of toothpaste is 10 cm long. We can also say that it is 1 dm long. The cap of the tube is about 1 cm long.

Estimate each length. Then measure to the nearest centimeter.

1.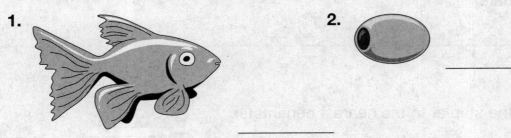

_____

2.

_____

3.

_____

4.

_____

5. **Number Sense** Estimate the length of your leg in centimeters. Then check your estimate.

_____

6. **Writing in Math** Kent says that half of a decimeter is about 3 cm. Do you agree? Explain.

_____

_____

Name_____

Centimeters and Decimeters

Estimate each length. Then measure to the nearest centimeter.

1.  _____

2.  _____

3. **Number Sense** Without using a ruler, draw a line that is 9 cm long. Check your estimate by measuring.

4. Estimate the perimeter of your desk in centimeters. Measure the perimeter to the nearest centimeter to check your estimate.

_____

Test Prep

5. Measure the stapler to the nearest centimeter.

   A. 2 cm   **B.** 3 cm

   C. 4 cm   **D.** 5 cm

6. **Writing in Math** Explain how you can find the number of centimeters in 6 dm.

_____

_____

_____

_____

Meters and Kilometers

A meter is 100 cm. A kilometer is 1,000 m.

• Centimeters, meters, and kilometers are the most commonly used metric measurements for length or distance.

• Centimeters are used to measure small items, like pencils and paper clips.

• Meters are used to measure larger items, like pieces of lumber. They are also used to measure small distances, such as the distance from the house to the garage.

• Kilometers are used to measure long distances, such as the distance between two towns.

Choose the best estimate for each.

1. the length of a truck _____   **A.** 4 cm

2. a screw _____   **B.** 4 m

3. a bike trail _____   **C.** 4 km

Tell if you would use meters or kilometers for each.

4. the distance to the next door neighbor's house _____

5. the perimeter of a basketball court _____

6. the length of a road _____

7. the length of a playground _____

8. the distance from Seattle to Chicago _____

Complete. Use patterns to find the missing numbers.

9.

m	10,000	7,000	5,000	1,000
km				1

10. **Number Sense** If you drove 8,000 m, how many kilometers did you drive? _____

Meters and Kilometers

Choose the best estimate for each.

1. a key _____   **A.** 3 km

2. height of a door _____   **B.** 3 m

3. distance to the store _____   **C.** 3 cm

Tell if you would use meters or kilometers for each.

4. diameter of Earth _____

5. length of a store aisle _____

6. distance of a bus route _____

7. The northern border of the United States is about
6,416 km. The Great Wall of China is 6,350 km long.
Which is longer, and by how many kilometers?

_____

_____

8. Complete. Use patterns to find the missing numbers.

m	1,000	3,000	5,000	7,000	9,000
km	1				

Test Prep

9. Which is the best estimate for the length of a person's nose?

     A. 5 ft   **B.** 5 cm   **C.** 5 m   **D.** 5 km

10. **Writing in Math** Is the length of your pencil greater than or
less than 1 m? Explain.

_____

_____

Name_____

Writing to Describe

Weight Lifting Barry lifts weights. Use the pattern to complete the table for Days 7 and 8.

Day	1	2	3	4	5	6	7	8
Amount lifted	80 lb	80 lb	85 lb	85 lb	90 lb	90 lb	95 lb	95 lb

Explain how the amount of weight Barry lifts changes as the number of days changes.

Tips for Writing a Math Explanation

- First, find a pattern.

- Tell how the pattern changes the number for each day.

- Use specific numbers as part of your explanation.

- Use words such as *increased* or *decreased.*

Barry lifted the same amount of weight for 2 days in a row, then increased the weight by 5 lb.

As each day increases by 1, the number of pounds either stays the same or increases by 5 lb.

On Day 7 Barry will lift 95 lb because when he increases the weight, he does so by 5 lb: 90 lb + 5 lb = 95 lb.

Because Barry keeps the weight the same for 2 days in a row, he will also lift 95 lb on Day 8.

---

1. Mary wraps gifts at a department store. She places 3 bows on each gift. Complete the table below to show how many bows she will need to wrap 5 and 6 gifts.

Number of Gifts	1	2	3	4	5	6
Bows	3	6	9	12		

Explain how the number of bows changes as the number of gifts changes.

_____

_____

Name_____

Writing to Explain

Write to explain.

1. Explain how a tenth is related to a hundredth.

_____

_____

_____

2. Explain how you can use three shapes
   to make the figure shown.

   _____

   _____

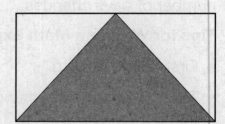

3. Explain how the 50 stars are arranged
   on the American flag.

   _____

   _____

4. Tell what part of the whole is shaded. Use tenths and
   hundredths in your explanation.

   _____

   _____

PROBLEM-SOLVING APPLICATION   **R 10-9**
Gudren's Quilts

Gudren sews quilts. The quilt she is currently sewing is made of
100 pieces of fabric. Each piece is the same size. How many
dark pieces of fabric will she need? Write a fraction and a
decimal for the shaded part of the quilt.

There are 64 dark pieces of fabric.

There are 100 squares, and 64 are shaded. So, sixty-four
hundredths are shaded.

Fraction: $\frac{64}{100}$ Decimal: 0.64

1. How many dark pieces of fabric will Gudren need for the
    quilt at the right? Write a fraction and a decimal for the
    shaded part.

_____

2. Gudren is deciding which rectangles to use for her next
    quilt. She has rectangles that are 0.32 in. long, 0.35 in.
    long, and 0.23 in. long. Write the lengths in order from least
    to greatest.

_____

3. Gudren wants to make a
    quilt for her nephew, who is
    5 years old. He loves
    alligators, so she wants to
    sew little alligator patches
    onto the quilt. How many
    centimeters long is each
    alligator patch?

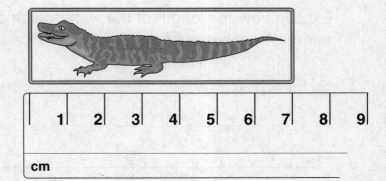

_____

Name_____

Friends of the Forests

1. The boundary of the forest near Steven's house is 7 km long. How many meters long is the boundary?

_____

2. The park in Cecilia's neighborhood has 3 different forest paths. Each path is about 400 m. Is the total of the 3 paths greater than or less than 1 km? Explain.

_____

_____

_____

In the United States, forests and woodlands make up three tenths of the land.

3. Write a decimal and fraction to show how much of the United States is forests and woodlands.   _____

4. Henry is cutting a 120 cm long watermelon into equal slices for his family's picnic. Each slice is 5 cm. Complete the table.

Number of Slices	0	1	2	3	4
Watermelon Length	120	115			

Explain how the length of the watermelon changes as the number of slices cut from the watermelon changes.

_____

_____

_____

Name_____

Mental Math: Multiplication Patterns

R 11-1

You can use multiplication patterns to help multiply multiples of 10 and 100.

When one of the factors you are multiplying has zeros on the end, you can multiply the nonzero digits, and then add on the extra zeros.

9 × 100

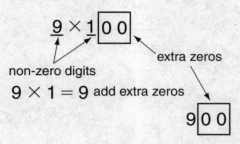

9 × 1 = 9 add extra zeros

9 × 100 = 900

12 × 2,000

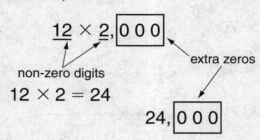

12 × 2 = 24

12 × 2,000 = 24,000

Use mental math to find each product.

1. 8 × 10 = _____

2. 7 × 100 = _____

3. 4 × 1,000 = _____

4. 3 × 50 = _____

5. 600 × 3 = _____

6. 4,000 × 7 = _____

Find the missing number in each number sentence.

7. ☐ × 100 = 600

8. 40 × ☐ = 360

9. Number Sense Karen says, "When I have a factor with exactly 2 zeros at the end, my answer will always have exactly 2 zeros at the end." Do you agree? Explain.

_____

_____

_____

_____

© Pearson Education, Inc. 3

138 Use with Lesson 11-1.

Mental Math:
Multiplication Patterns

Use mental math to find each product.

1. $3 \times 10 =$ _____ **2.** $6 \times 100 =$ _____

3. $9 \times 1,000 =$ _____ **4.** $80 \times 3 =$ _____

5. $4 \times 700 =$ _____ **6.** $2,000 \times 5 =$ _____

7. $6 \times 400 =$ _____ **8.** $800 \times 8 =$ _____

9. $600 \times 9 =$ _____

Algebra Find the missing number in each number sentence.

10. $9 \times$ _____ $= 720$ **11.** _____ $\times 5,000 = 40,000$

12. The average workweek is 40 hr. How many
hours are there in 4 workweeks? _____

13. There are 2,000 lb in 1 T. How many pounds
are there in 16 T? _____

14. Lightning strikes the earth about 200 times
each second. How many times does lightning
strike the earth in 1 min? _____

Test Prep

15. How many hundreds are there in 2,000?

   A. 2,000   **B.** 200   **C.** 20   **D.** 2

16. **Writing in Math** Explain how to use mental math to find 700×8.

_____

_____

_____

Name_____

Estimating Products

R 11-2

You can use rounding to estimate products.

Estimate 6 × 22.

Round 22 to the nearest ten.

6 × 22
   ↓ 22 rounds
     to 20.
6 × 20 = 120

6 × 22 is about 120.

Estimate 8 × 387.

Round 387 to the nearest hundred.

8 × 387
   ↓ 387 rounds
     to 400.
8 × 400 = 3,200

8 × 387 is about 3,200.

Estimate each product.

1. 8 × 91 _____

2. 4 × 689 _____

3. 3 × 53 _____

4. 2 × 2114 _____

5. 7 × 67 _____

6. 9 × 634 _____

7. 8 × 7,984 _____

8. 5 × 362 _____

9. 8 × 5,021 _____

10. 9 × 2,753 _____

11. 6 × 3,103 _____

12. 7 × 8,789 _____

13. Number Sense Is 4 × 857 less than 3,750? How do you know?

_____

_____

_____

_____

14. The Moon orbits Earth about every 27 days.
For the Moon to orbit 9 times, will it take more
than 300 days? _____

Estimating Products

Estimate each product.

1. 4×869 _____

2. 7×41 _____

3. $3 \times 6,872$ _____

4. 2×631 _____

5. 5×98 _____

6. $9 \times 8,127$ _____

7. 6×38 _____

8. 8×767 _____

9. **Number Sense** Cheryl has 3 weeks to finish a project. She knows that she can spend 2 hr a day on the project, and that it will take her about 40 hr. If Cheryl works on the project every day, does she have enough time to finish it?

_____

_____

_____

10. There are 365 days in 1 year. About how many days are there in 7 years?

_____

Test Prep

11. Which is the best estimate for 7×419?

   A. 2,100   **B.** 2,800   **C.** 3,500   **D.** 4,000

12. **Writing in Math** There are 5,280 ft in 1 mi. Explain how you can tell if there are at least 25,000 ft in 5 mi.

_____

_____

_____

Mental Math: Division Patterns

When there are zeros at the end of the dividend, you can move them aside and use a basic division fact to divide the nonzero digits.

For example:

120 ÷ 4

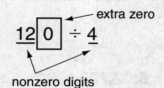

extra zero

nonzero digits

12 ÷ 4 = 3 add extra zero 30

So, 120 ÷ 4 = 30.

Remember to add the same number of zeros back to the quotient that you removed from the dividend.

6⬚0⬚ ÷ 3 = 2⬚0⬚   1 zero

6⬚0 0⬚ ÷ 3 = 2⬚0 0⬚   2 zeros

6,⬚0 0 0⬚ ÷ 3 = 2,⬚0 0 0⬚   3 zeros

Use patterns to find each quotient.

1. 24 ÷ 4 = _____   **2.** 240 ÷ 4 = _____   **3.** 2,400 ÷ 4 = _____

Use mental math to find each quotient.

4. 250 ÷ 5 = _____   **5.** 180 ÷ 6 = _____   **6.** 3,200 ÷ 8 = _____

7. 900 ÷ 3 = _____   **8.** 800 ÷ 8 = _____   **9.** 280 ÷ 7 = _____

10. Number Sense There are 200 school days that are divided into 4 equal grading periods. How many school days are in each grading period?

_____

Name_____

Mental Math: Division Patterns

Use patterns to find each quotient.

1. 18 ÷ 3 = _____

180 ÷ 3 = _____

1,800 ÷ 3 = _____

2. 36 ÷ 4 = _____

360 ÷ 4 = _____

3,600 ÷ 4 = _____

Use mental math to find each quotient.

3. 200 ÷ 5 = _____

4. 3,600 ÷ 6 = _____

5. 2,700 ÷ 3 = _____

6. 490 ÷ 7 = _____

7. 1,200 ÷ 2 = _____

8. 630 ÷ 9 = _____

Algebra Use mental math to find the missing numbers.

9. 810 ÷ _____ = 90

10. _____ ÷ 2 = 800

11. _____ ÷ 7 = 500

12. 4,200 ÷ _____ = 600

13. There are 5 reams of paper in a box. There are 2,500 pages total in the box. How many sheets of paper are in 1 ream of paper?

_____

Test Prep

14. Use mental math to find the quotient of 480 ÷ 8.

A. 6 **B.** 8 **C.** 60 **D.** 80

15. Writing in Math Explain how you can find the quotient for 120,000 ÷ 3 using mental math.

_____

_____

_____

_____

Estimating Quotients

When you know the basic division facts, you can estimate the quotient of a division problem.

Estimate $19 \div 3$.

First, think about the basic facts that you know that use the same divisor, 3.

For example:

$12 \div 3 = 4$ $15 \div 3 = 5$

$18 \div 3 = 6$ $21 \div 3 = 7$

Then choose the basic fact that has the closest dividend to the problem you are solving.

19 is between the dividends of 18 and 21. It is closer to 18, so use the basic fact $18 \div 3 = 6$.

So, $19 \div 3$ is about 6.

Estimate each quotient.

1. $34 \div 8$ _____   2. $22 \div 3$ _____   3. $46 \div 5$ _____

4. $15 \div 8$ _____   5. $17 \div 6$ _____   6. $58 \div 7$ _____

7. $43 \div 9$ _____   8. $35 \div 4$ _____   9. $74 \div 24$ _____

10. **Reasoning** There are 12 eggs and 5 people. If each person eats the same number of eggs, did each person eat at least 3 eggs? Explain.

_____

_____

_____

Name_____

Estimating Quotients

P 11-4

Estimate each quotient.

1. 66 ÷ 8 _____ 2. 31 ÷ 6 _____

3. 19 ÷ 2 _____ 4. 23 ÷ 4 _____

5. 22 ÷ 6 _____ 6. 43 ÷ 7 _____

7. 70 ÷ 8 _____ 8. 19 ÷ 4 _____

9. A group of students is sharing 62 markers. If there are 7 students, about how many markers will each student have?

_____

10. James has 6 pencils. His father has 44 pencils. About how many times more pencils does James's father have?

_____

11. **Number Sense** Without finding the exact answer, how do you know that 41 ÷ 5 is greater than 40 ÷ 5?

_____

_____

Test Prep

12. Which is the best estimate for 37 ÷ 5?

   A. 5   **B.** 6   **C.** 7   **D.** 8

13. **Writing in Math** Frances has 37 c of apples to make loaves of apple bread. If each loaf uses 4 c of apples, explain how Frances can find about how many loaves she can make.

_____

_____

© Pearson Education, Inc. 3

Use with Lesson 11-4. **141**

Multiplication and Arrays

You can draw a picture of an array to show multiplication.

For example:

4×21

What You Show	**What You Think**
	4 rows of 2 tens = 8 tens
	4 rows of 1 ones = 4 ones
	80 + 4 = 84

To find the product, count the tens and the ones, then add them together.

There are 8 tens and 4 ones.

8 tens = 80, 4 ones = 4

80 + 4 = 84

So, $4 \times 21 = 84$.

Find each product. You may draw a picture to help.

1. $3 \times 14 = $ _____

2. $2 \times 23 = $ _____   3. $4 \times 17 = $ _____

4. $3 \times 18 = $ _____   5. $2 \times 34 = $ _____

6. **Number Sense** Suppose you wanted to draw an array for 21×3. How many ones would you draw? _____

Name_____

Multiplication and Arrays

Find each product. You may draw a picture to help.

1. 3 × 17 = _____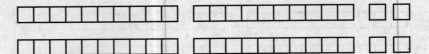

2. 2 × 22 = _____

3. 5 × 34 = _____   **4.** 4 × 13 = _____   **5.** 3 × 57 = _____

6. Reasoning Draw an array to show the number
of eggs in 3 dozens.
_____

Each worker is paid $8 per hour of work.

Worker	Hours Worked
Bob	19
Josh	35
Marvin	13

7. How many dollars did Bob earn?

_____

8. How many dollars did Josh earn?   _____

9. How much more did Bob earn than Marvin?   _____

Test Prep

10. Which is the product of 52 × 6?

   A. 42   **B.** 302   **C.** 312   **D.** 402

11. Writing in Math Explain how to use an array to find 3 × 19.

_____

Breaking Numbers Apart to Multiply

You can make multiplication easier by breaking larger numbers apart by place value.

Find 4×23.

23 is the same as $20 + 3$.

First multiply the ones, then multiply the tens.

$4 \times 20 = 80$	$4 \times 3 = 12$

Then add the products together. $80 + 12 = 92$

So, $4 \times 23 = 92$.

Find each product.

1.   21
   $\times\ 6$

2.   43
   $\times\ 5$

3.   16
   $\times\ 8$

4. $38
   $\times\ 9$

5. $62 \times 4 =$ _____

6. $2 \times 19 =$ _____

7. $4 \times 22 =$ _____

8. $5 \times 21 =$ _____

9. Number Sense Tim said, "To find 6×33, I can add 18 and 18."
   Do you agree with him? Why or why not?

_____

_____

_____

Breaking Numbers Apart to Multiply   P 11-6

Find each product.

1.   63
   × 4

2.   18
   × 7

3. $42
   × 9

4.   88
   × 2

5. 2 × 72 = _____

6. 3 × 49 = _____

7. 6 × 31 = _____

8. 3 × 82 = _____

9. Each wood panel is 6 ft wide. Exactly 19 panels
   are needed to cover the walls of a room. What is
   the perimeter of the room?

   _____

10. A carpenter makes chairs with slats that run
    across the back of the chairs as shown. Each
    chair uses 7 slats. He needs to make 36 chairs.
    How many slats must he make?

Slats

    _____

Test Prep

11. Which is the same as 5 × 25?

    A. 25 + 10   B. 105   C. 30   D. 100 + 25

12. **Writing in Math** Susie says, "I can find 12 × 8 by adding
    80 and 16." Do you agree? Why or why not?

    _____

    _____

    _____

    _____

    _____

Multiplying Two-Digit Numbers

You can regroup tens and ones to multiply two-digit numbers.

Find 36×3.

	What You Think	**What You Write**

Step 1

Multiply the ones. Regroup if necessary.
$6 \times 3 = 18$ ones. Regroup 18 ones as 1 ten 8 ones.

$$\begin{array}{r} 1 \\ 3\,6 \\ \times \quad 3 \\ \hline 8 \end{array}$$

Step 2

Multiply the tens. Add any regrouped tens.
3×3 tens $= 9$ tens.
9 tens $+$ 1 ten $= 10$ tens.

$$\begin{array}{r} 1 \\ 3\,6 \\ \times \quad 3 \\ \hline 1\,0\,8 \end{array}$$

So, $36 \times 3 = 108$.

Find each product. Decide if your answer is reasonable.

1.
$$\begin{array}{r} 21 \\ \times \quad 6 \\ \hline \end{array}$$

2.
$$\begin{array}{r} 14 \\ \times \quad 3 \\ \hline \end{array}$$

3.
$$\begin{array}{r} 32 \\ \times \quad 4 \\ \hline \end{array}$$

4.
$$\begin{array}{r} 57 \\ \times \quad 5 \\ \hline \end{array}$$

5.
$$\begin{array}{r} 62 \\ \times \quad 8 \\ \hline \end{array}$$

6.
$$\begin{array}{r} 33 \\ \times \quad 5 \\ \hline \end{array}$$

7. $43 \times 8 = $ _____

8. $28 \times 6 = $ _____

9. $43 \times 2 = $ _____

10. Number Sense The largest snowman on record was almost 38 yd tall. There are 3 ft in a yard. How many feet are in 38 yd?

_____

Name_____

Multiplying Two-Digit Numbers

Find each product. Decide if your answer is reasonable.

1. $\begin{array}{r} 12 \\ \times\ \ 9 \\ \hline \end{array}$

2. $\begin{array}{r} 19 \\ \times\ \ 4 \\ \hline \end{array}$

3. $\begin{array}{r} \$22 \\ \times\ \ \ 7 \\ \hline \end{array}$

4. $\begin{array}{r} 45 \\ \times\ \ 6 \\ \hline \end{array}$

5. $\begin{array}{r} 96 \\ \times\ \ 3 \\ \hline \end{array}$

6. $\begin{array}{r} 27 \\ \times\ \ 5 \\ \hline \end{array}$

7. $\begin{array}{r} 12 \\ \times\ \ 8 \\ \hline \end{array}$

8. $\begin{array}{r} \$55 \\ \times\ \ \ 4 \\ \hline \end{array}$

9. $\begin{array}{r} 9 \\ \times\ \$36 \\ \hline \end{array}$

10. $\begin{array}{r} 37 \\ \times\ \ 4 \\ \hline \end{array}$

11. $\begin{array}{r} 82 \\ \times\ \ 6 \\ \hline \end{array}$

12. $\begin{array}{r} \$71 \\ \times\ \ \ 7 \\ \hline \end{array}$

13. $14 \times 5 =$ _____

14. $6 \times 51 =$ _____

15. $63 \times 4 =$ _____

16. $\$47 \times 2 =$ _____

17. An area in Norway gets sunlight all day for 14 weeks straight during the summer. How many days of continuous sunlight is this?

_____

18. The length of a parking lot is 92 yd. How many feet long is the parking lot?

_____

Test Prep

19. Which is the product of $82 \times \$7$?

   A. $434   **B.** $494   **C.** $564   **D.** $574

20. **Writing in Math** Explain how an array of 5×46 can help you find the product of 5×46.

_____

_____

_____

Name_____

Multiplying Three-Digit Numbers

A three-digit factor is multiplied the same way a two-digit factor is.

Find 523 × 7.

Step 1	**Step 2**	**Step 3**
Multiply the ones. Regroup if needed.	Multiply the tens. Add any extra tens. Regroup if needed.	Multiply the hundreds. Add any extra hundreds.
$\begin{array}{r} \overset{2}{} \\ 5\,2\,3 \\ \times\quad 7 \\ \hline 1 \end{array}$	$\begin{array}{r} \overset{1}{}\overset{2}{} \\ 5\,2\,3 \\ \times\quad 7 \\ \hline 6\,1 \end{array}$	$\begin{array}{r} \overset{1}{}\overset{2}{} \\ 5\,2\,3 \\ \times\quad 7 \\ \hline 3,6\,6\,1 \end{array}$

Estimate to check. 523 × 7 = 500 × 7 = 3,500.
3,661 is close to 3,500, so the answer is reasonable.

Remember, it is important to always start with the ones place, and work from the least place value to the greatest. Any regrouping needs to be done going from least to greatest.

Find each answer. Estimate to check reasonableness.

1. $\begin{array}{r} 221 \\ \times\quad 4 \\ \hline \end{array}$ 2. $\begin{array}{r} 342 \\ \times\quad 5 \\ \hline \end{array}$ 3. $\begin{array}{r} 402 \\ \times\quad 4 \\ \hline \end{array}$

4. $\begin{array}{r} 610 \\ \times\quad 2 \\ \hline \end{array}$ 5. $\begin{array}{r} 531 \\ \times\quad 3 \\ \hline \end{array}$ 6. $\begin{array}{r} 213 \\ \times\quad 8 \\ \hline \end{array}$

7. 392 × 6 = _____   8. 104 × 9 = _____

9. **Number Sense** The Tonga micro-plate near Samoa moves at a rate of 240 mm each year. At that rate, how many millimeters will the plate have moved in 5 years?

_____

_____

© Pearson Education, Inc. 3

Use with Lesson 11-8. **145**

Multiplying Three-Digit Numbers

Find each answer. Estimate to check reasonableness.

1. 231
   × 2

2. 420
   × 3

3. 613
   × 5

4. 122
   × 8

5. 308
   × 7

6. 501
   × 8

7. 727
   × 4

8. 914
   × 9

9. $444 \times 4 =$ _____

10. $121 \times 6 =$ _____

11. There are 365 days in 1 year. How many days
    are there in 3 years?   _____

12. A board is 144 in. long. How many inches long
    are 8 boards?   _____

13. **Number Sense** Is 721×3 the same as $2,100 + 60 + 3$? Explain.

_____

_____

Test Prep

14. Which is the product of 828×5?

    A. 4,040   **B.** 4,100   **C.** 4,140   **D.** 4,840

15. **Writing in Math** Larry multiplied 362×4.
    Explain Larry's error and give the correct answer.

    $$\begin{array}{r} {}^{2}\,362 \\ \times\ 4 \\ \hline 1,248 \end{array}$$

_____

_____

Name_____

Multiplying Money

The only difference between multiplying money and whole numbers is the final step. The answer must be written in the form of money. Make sure you put in the dollar sign ($) and the decimal point.

For example:

Find $7.36 × 7.

Step 1	**Step 2**
Multiply the same way as with whole numbers.	Write the answer in dollars and cents.

$$\begin{array}{r} 2\ \ 4 \\ \$7\ .\ 3\ 6 \\ \times\qquad 7 \\ \hline 5\ 1\ \ 5\ 2 \end{array}$$

$$\begin{array}{r} 2\ \ 4 \\ \$7\ .\ 3\ 6 \\ \times\qquad 7 \\ \hline \$5\ 1\ .\ 5\ 2 \end{array}$$

Estimate to check. 7 × $7.36 = 7 × 7 = 49
$51.52 is close to 49, so the answer is reasonable.

Find each product. Estimate to check reasonableness.

1.	$1.25	2.	$6.98	3.	$4.24	4.	$3.42
	× 3		× 2		× 5		× 8

5. Kirk bought 3 roast beef sandwiches. How much did it cost?

_____

6. If you bought 7 tuna sandwiches, how much would it cost?

_____

Lunch Menu	
Tuna Sandwich	$4.53
Roast Beef Sandwich	$5.15
Chips	$1.28
Drink	$1.14

7. **Number Sense** Write a multiplication sentence with a 3-digit number that does not require regrouping.

_____

Name_____

Multiplying Money

Find each product. Estimate to check reasonableness.

1. $1.32
   $\times$ 6

2. $4.67
   $\times$ 4

3. $6.04
   $\times$ 9

4. $4.21
   $\times$ 2

5. $7.49
   $\times$ 3

6. $5.08
   $\times$ 7

7. $8.29
   $\times$ 3

8. $5.65
   $\times$ 8

9. $6.78 $\times$ 1 = _____

10. $7.90 $\times$ 4 = _____

11. $3.22 $\times$ 5 = _____

12. How much is 4 gal of milk?

_____

13. How much is 6 bagels?

_____

14. How much is 7 gal of gas?

_____

```
┌──────────────────────────────┐
│  Fast Gas                     │
│  Gas/gallon        $1.37      │
│ ─────────────────────────────│
│  Come inside!                 │
│  Milk gallon  ..........  $2.49 │
│  Bread  ................  $0.99 │
│  Bagels  ..............  2/$1.89│
└──────────────────────────────┘
```

Test Prep

15. If wallpaper is $8.27 a roll, which is the cost of 8 rolls?

   A. $48.62   **B.** $62.76   **C.** $66.16   **D.** $78.22

16. **Writing in Math** Explain how to find the product of
    $7.50 $\times$ 8.

_____

_____

Name _____

Choose a Computation Method

If the answer is easy to find, you can use mental math. Use mental math for problems like:

$90 \div 9$ or $3,000 \times 7$.

If the answer is not too difficult to find, and there are not many regroupings, use paper and pencil. Use paper and pencil for problems like:

$912 \div 3$ or 62×4 or $615 + 88$.

For problems that have a lot of regroupings, a calculator is a good choice. Some problems that you might choose a calculator to solve are:

$15,328 \times 37$ or $8,921,320 \div 8$.

Find each product. Tell which computation method you used.

1. 3,000
      $\times$ 4

2. 189
      $\times$ 2

3. $302
      $\times$ 9

4. $5,887 \times 6 =$ _____

5. $\$421 \times 3 =$ _____

6. $\$500 \times 7 =$ _____

7. Writing in Math Why is mental math not a good method to use when finding $6,789 \times 5$?

_____

_____

_____

Name_____

Choose a Computation Method

Find each product. Tell which computation method you used.

1. $9.07
    ×   4
    _____

2. 500
    ×   3
    _____

3. 3,678
    ×   9
    _____

4. 619
    ×   7
    _____

5. 7,234 × 7 = _____

_____

6. 8,000 × 4 = _____

7. **Number Sense** Explain which computation method you
   would choose to multiply $4.32 × 6.

_____

_____

8. Celia sent 4 packages out through the mail. Three
   of them had postage of $6.32 and one was $7.51.
   How much was the postage altogether? _____

Test Prep

9. Which is the product of 811 × 9?

   A. 72,990   **B.** 7,299   **C.** 7,209   **D.** 7,200

10. **Writing in Math** Explain when it is best to use a calculator
    to solve a problem.

_____

_____

_____

_____

PROBLEM-SOLVING STRATEGY   **R 11-11**

Use Logical Reasoning

Age Carla is 18 years old. Her father is 4 years older than her mother. Carla's mother is twice as old as Carla. How old is Carla's father?

Read and Understand

Step 1: What do you know?

Carla's age is 18. Carla's mother is twice Carla's age. Her father is 4 years older than her mother.

Step 2: What are you trying to find?

Carla's father's age

Plan and Solve

Step 3: What strategy will you use?

Strategy: Use logical reasoning

Draw a picture to help organize what you know.

Carla's mother is twice Carla's age, or 2 × 18 = 36. So, Carla's mother is 36. Carla's father is 4 years older than her mother, or 36 + 4 = 40. So, Carla's father is 40 years old.

Look Back and Check

Step 4: Is your work correct?

Yes, all the clues match the answer.

Solve. Write the answer in a complete sentence.

1. Complete the table to decide what color house Peter lives in.

   Clues:
   • Tom does not live in a blue house.
   • Willis likes his white house.

	Peter	**Tom**	**Willis**
Blue			
Green			
White			

   _____

   _____

148   Use with Lesson 11-11.

PROBLEM-SOLVING STRATEGY

Use Logical Reasoning

Solve. Write the answer in a complete sentence.

1. Complete the table. Then use the table to find what color uniform the Wolves wear.

_____

   - The Bears do not wear red or green.
   - The Cougars wear white.
   - There is no green on the Pumas' uniforms.

	Bears	Cougars	Pumas	Wolves
Blue				
Green				
Red				
White				

2. Sally has an appointment on Thursday. The first appointment of the day is at 9 A.M. and the final one is at 3 P.M. Sally's appointment is not the first of the day or the last. Her appointment is on the hour. The sum of the digits in the hour is 3. What time is Sally's appointment?

_____

3. I am an odd number with 3 digits. The sum of my digits is 5. My first and last digits are the same. What number am I?

_____

4. Ben's grandfather is 5 times as old as Ben. Ben's father is 22 years younger than his grandfather. If Ben is 12 years old, how old is Ben's father?

_____

Name_____

Using Objects to Divide

How to use place-value blocks to show division with greater numbers:

Find 45 ÷ 3.

Step 1	**Step 2**	**Step 3**
Use place-value blocks to show 45. Draw 3 circles to show how many equal groups you will make.	Divide the tens. Put an equal number of tens in each circle. There is 1 ten left over.	Regroup the leftover tens as ones. 1 ten = 10 ones. Combine them with the ones that were already there. Place an equal number of ones in each circle.

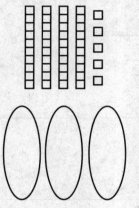 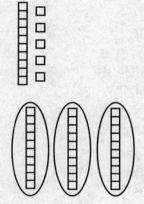

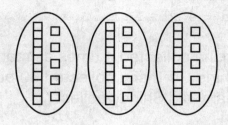

I can put 1 ten and 5 ones in each group. 1 ten + 5 ones = 15. So 45 ÷ 3 = 15.

Use place-value blocks or draw a picture to find each quotient.

1. 46 ÷ 2 = _____

2. 48 ÷ 4 = _____

3. 72 ÷ 3 = _____

4. 39 ÷ 3 = _____

5. 60 ÷ 4 = _____

6. 98 ÷ 7 = _____

7. 88 ÷ 4 = _____

8. 51 ÷ 3 = _____

9. 57 ÷ 3 = _____

10. 96 ÷ 6 = _____

11. **Number Sense** Tim's mom is packing fruit bars for her 3 sons to take on a campout. She has 36 mini-sized bars. How many bars will each son have packed?

_____

Using Objects to Divide

Use place-value blocks or draw a picture to find each quotient.

1. $64 \div 4 =$ _____

2. $94 \div 2 =$ _____

3. $51 \div 3 =$ _____

4. $80 \div 5 =$ _____

5. $91 \div 7 =$ _____

6. $80 \div 8 =$ _____

7. $96 \div 8 =$ _____

8. $87 \div 3 =$ _____

9. $88 \div 4 =$ _____

10. $57 \div 3 =$ _____

11. Trisha collected 4 times as many bugs as Shirley. If Trisha collected 60 bugs, how many did Shirley collect?

_____

12. Candice bought a box of books for $78. There are 6 books in a box. If they all cost the same, how much did each book cost?

_____

Test Prep

13. Which is the quotient of $630 \div 9$?

   A. 7   **B.** 8   **C.** 60   **D.** 70

14. **Writing in Math** Explain how you could use a picture to help you solve $81 \div 3$.

_____

_____

_____

_____

_____

Name_____

Breaking Numbers Apart to Divide   R 11-13

You can break apart numbers into groups of tens and ones to divide.

Find 42 ÷ 2.

Step 1 Break apart 42 into tens and ones.

42 is the same as 4 tens and 2 ones.

42 = 40 + 2

Step 2 Divide the tens, then divide the ones.

Tens: 40 ÷ 2 = 20

Ones: 2 ÷ 2 = 1

Step 3 Add the two quotients.

20 + 1 = 21

So, 42 ÷ 2 = 21.

Use the break apart method to find each quotient. You may draw a picture to help.

1. 55 ÷ 5 = _____

2. 48 ÷ 4 = _____

3. 82 ÷ 2 = _____

4. 3)93

5. 2)46

6. 3)66

7. 63 ÷ 3 = _____

8. 88 ÷ 4 = _____

9. 24 ÷ 2 = _____

10. 4)44

11. 3)96

12. 6)66

13. **Number Sense** Niko has 28 pencils. He is putting them evenly into two drawers. How many pencils will be in each drawer?

_____

Name_____

Breaking Numbers Apart to Divide   P 11-13

Use the break apart method to find each quotient. You may draw a picture to help.

1. $60 \div 3 =$ _____

2. $60 \div 4 =$ _____

3. $72 \div 3 =$ _____

4. $95 \div 5 =$ _____

5. $4\overline{)64}$ 6. $2\overline{)64}$ 7. $2\overline{)32}$ 8. $3\overline{)48}$

9. Jennifer has 57 fish in one tank. She wants to move them to 3 smaller tanks. If she puts the same number of fish in each of the 3 smaller tanks, how many fish will be in each tank?

_____

10. There is enough room for 5 rows of chairs in a room. There are 75 people to be seated. How many chairs must be in each row?

_____

Test Prep

11. Which has the greatest quotient?

    A. $75 \div 3$ **B.** $96 \div 4$ **C.** $82 \div 2$ **D.** $48 \div 3$

12. **Writing in Math** Explain how using the break apart method can help you solve $84 \div 4$.

_____

_____

_____

_____

© Pearson Education, Inc. 3

150   Use with Lesson 11-13.

Dividing

Find 51 ÷ 3.

	What You Think	**What You Write**
Step 1	Divide the tens. 5 tens ÷ 3 = 1 ten with 2 tens left over.	$\begin{array}{r} 1 \\ 3\overline{)51} \\ -\ 3 \\ \hline 2 \end{array}$ ← 1 ten in each group ← (3 × 1) tens used ← 2 tens left over
Step 2	Regroup the tens as ones. 2 tens = 20 ones. Combine with the 1 one already there.	$\begin{array}{r} 1 \\ 3\overline{)51} \\ -\ 3\downarrow \\ \hline 21 \end{array}$ Bring down the 1 one. 21 ones in all
Step 3	Divide the ones.	$\begin{array}{r} 17 \\ 3\overline{)51} \\ -\ 3 \\ \hline 21 \\ -\ 21 \\ \hline 0 \end{array}$ ← 17 ones in each group ← (7 × 3) ones used ← 0 ones left over

Complete. Check your answer.

1.
```
    1 □
  4)6 8
  - 4↓
  ───
   □ 8
  -□□
  ───
    □
```

2.
```
   2 □
  3)8 4
 -□□
 ───
  □ 4
 -□□
 ───
   □
```
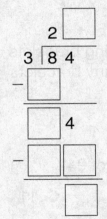

3.
```
  □ □
 2)9 4
 -□□
 ───
 □□
 -□□
 ───
  □
```
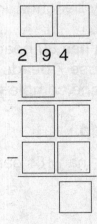

Divide. Check your answers.

4. 73 ÷ 2 = _____   5. 63 ÷ 3 = _____   6. 96 ÷ 8 = _____

7. **Number Sense** If you divide 20 ÷ 5, will there be a remainder? How do you know?

_____

_____

Name_____

Dividing

P 11-14

Complete. Check your answer.

1.

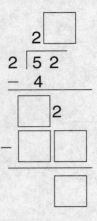

2.

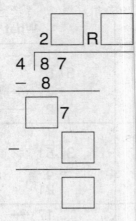

3.

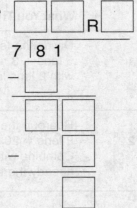

Divide. Check your answers.

4. 7)91   **5.** 4)35   **6.** 5)46   **7.** 2)71

8. A set of bleachers will seat 72 people. If each bench in the bleachers seats 6 people, how many benches are there?

_____

9. Lana has 80 beads. She is making bracelets that use 7 beads each. How many bracelets can she complete?

_____

Test Prep

10. How many 8s can you take out of 94?

   A. 13   **B.** 12   **C.** 11   **D.** 10

11. Writing in Math Maureen divided 72 by 3. Is her work correct? If not, tell why and give the correct answer.

```
  1 1 4
3)7 2
  3
  ‾‾‾
  4 2
  4 2
  ‾‾‾
    0
```

_____

_____

_____

_____

© Pearson Education, Inc. 3

Use with Lesson 11-14. **151**

Name_____

Interpreting Remainders

Window Repair Sam repairs broken windows. It takes him about 4 hr to repair 1 window. He works 25 hr each week.

How many windows are repaired in 1 week?	How many windows will be worked on in 1 week?	How many hours will be spent working on the seventh window in 1 work week?
Plan and Solve	**Plan and Solve**	**Plan and Solve**
6 R1 4)25 − 24 1	6 R1 4)25 − 24 1	6 R1 4)25 − 24 1
6 windows can be repaired.	7 windows will be worked on.	1 hr will be spent on the last window.
Look Back and Check	**Look Back and Check**	**Look Back and Check**
The 1 hr left over is not enough to repair another window.	He will begin working on the seventh window in the remaining 1 hr.	4 windows are repaired in 24 hr. There is 1 more hour in the work week.

Solve. Write the answer in a complete sentence.

1. Tanya is knitting baby sweaters. Each sweater needs 5 balls of yarn. She has 34 balls of yarn. How many sweaters can she make?

_____

2. José had $34. He bought as many packages of socks as he could. The socks cost $5 a package. How much money did José have left after he bought the socks? How much more money does he need to buy another package of socks?

_____

_____

Interpreting Remainders

Use the table for 1–4.

Gail is a plumber. She is going to buy some supplies at the hardware store.

Item	Number in Package	Cost per Package
Nails	50	$3.00
Screws	25	$6.00
1 in. copper elbow	3	$2.50
1 in. pipe – 6 ft	1	$5.00

1. How many packages of copper elbows should Gail buy if she needs 41 elbows?

   _____

2. How many packages of nails can Gail buy with $74.00?

   _____

3. How many packages of screws can Gail buy with $52.00?

   _____

4. If Gail started with $76.00 and bought as many pipes as she could, how much money would she have left?

   _____

5. Skyler has 47 apples. There are 3 people in his family. If each person ate the same number of apples, how many have they each eaten? How many apples are left?

   _____

   _____

PROBLEM-SOLVING APPLICATION   **R 11-16**
The Volleyball Team

Volleyball Team The elementary school has just started a volleyball team, and 42 girls signed up. They would like to have at least 1 coach for every 8 girls. How many volleyball coaches are needed?

$$\begin{array}{r} 5 \\ 8\overline{)42} \\ -40 \\ \hline 2 \end{array}$$

$42 \div 8 = 5\ R2$

There are 2 girls left without a coach. So I need to have at least one more coach if I want to have no more than 8 girls to each coach.

So, 6 coaches are needed.

1. Lydia is buying caps for the girls on her volleyball squad. The caps cost $3.99 each. There are 7 girls on Lydia's squad. How much will Lydia spend? _____

2. Sara, Cheryl, and Joan each have a different-colored shirt on. Their shirts are red, blue, and pink. Cheryl is not wearing pink, and Sara is wearing red. What color is Joan's shirt?

_____

3. There are 4 rows left in the auditorium. Each row has 18 seats in it. There are 3 classes that still need to be seated. There are 23, 27, and 24 students in the classes. Will there be enough seats?

_____

4. A team is having an end-of-season party at a local restaurant. There are 19 people coming, and the tables each seat 4. How many tables do they need to reserve?

_____

Name_____

Sleep Time

Solve. Write the answer in a complete sentence.

Average Sleep per Day

Animal	Hours
Elephant	2
Gorilla	14
Human	8
Sloth	18

1. How many minutes does a human sleep per day?

   _____

2. How many hours does an elephant sleep per year?

   _____

3. How many hours does a sloth sleep per week?

   _____

4. How many days will it take for a human to sleep 99 hr?

   _____

   _____

5. Midge is leaving for a trip in June. It is not on a weekday. The sum of the date's digits is 8. On what date is Midge leaving for her trip?

June						
S	M	T	W	T	F	S
		1	2	3	4	5
6	7	8	9	10	11	12
13	14	15	16	17	18	19
20	21	22	23	24	25	26
27	28	29	30			

   _____

   _____

Name_____

Customary Units of Capacity

Capacity is the amount of liquid a container can hold. The customary system measures capacity in cups, pints, quarts, and gallons, from smallest to largest.

2 cups (c) = 1 pint (pt)

2 pints (pt) = 1 quart (qt)

4 quarts (qt) = 1 gallon (gal)

4 gal = _____ qt

You are going from a large unit (gallons) to a smaller unit (quarts), so you are going to use multiplication. There are 4 qt in 1 gal.

Multiply the number of gallons by 4 to find the number of quarts.

4 gal × 4 = 16

4 gal = 16 qt

6 c = _____ pt

You are going from a smaller unit (cups) to a larger unit (pints), so you are going to use division.

There are 2 c in 1 pt.

Divide the number of cups by 2 to find the number of pints.

6 c ÷ 2 = 3

6 c = 3 pt

Estimate Choose the better estimate for each.

1.  1 c or 1 gal

_____

2.  1 qt or 1 c

_____

Find each missing number.

3. 3 gal = _____ qt

4. 4 pt = _____ qt

5. 4 pt = _____ c

6. 5 qt = _____ pt

7. 10 c = _____ pt

8. 20 qt = _____ gal

Name _____

Customary Units of Capacity

Estimate Choose the better estimate for each.

1.

   1 c or 1 gal _____

2.

   3 pt or 3 qt _____

Find the missing number.

3. 2 gal = _____ qt   4. 8 qt = _____ pt   5. 32 c = _____ gal

6. 12 pt = _____ qt   7. 5 gal = _____ pt   8. 2 qt = _____ c

9. Which is less, 7 c of water or 3 qt of water?   _____

10. **Number Sense** How many cups are in 1 qt 1 pt?   _____

11. A 10 gal fish tank with 12 fish in it needs $\frac{1}{2}$ of its water
    replaced every 2 weeks. How many quarts of water need
    to be replaced?   _____

12. There is about 10 pt of blood in the human body. How
    many quarts of blood are there?   _____

Test Prep

13. How many gallons are there in 40 qt?

    A. 160   **B.** 80   **C.** 20   **D.** 10

14. **Writing in Math** Explain how you found the answer for
    Exercise 11.

    _____

    _____

    _____

154 Use with Lesson 12-1.

Milliliters and Liters

Milliliters (mL) are commonly used to measure very small amounts of liquid. There are 5 mL in 1 tsp.

A liter is a little more than 1 qt. 1 L = 1,000 mL. Many beverages, such as sports drinks, spring water, and soda, are packaged in 1 or 2 L bottles.

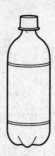

How to change between liters and milliliters:

7,000 mL = _____ L

You know that 1,000 mL = 1 L, so 7,000 mL = 7 × 1 L.

7,000 mL = 7 L

8 L = _____ mL

You know that 1 L = 1,000 mL, so 8 L = 8 × 1,000 mL.

8 L = 8,000 mL

Estimation Choose the better estimate for each.

1.    100 mL or 10 L

2.    3 L or 30 mL

_____   _____

3. Which is more, 2,500 mL of milk or 3 L of milk?

_____

4. Which is less, 4 L of soup or 400 mL of soup?

_____

Name_____

Milliliters and Liters

Estimation Choose the better estimate for each.

1.

250 mL or 1 L _____

2.

4 L or 40 mL _____

3. Which is less, 3,500 mL of oil or 3 L of oil? _____

Compare. Use >, <, or =.

4. 10 L ◯ 10,000 mL

5. 8,000 mL ◯ 7 L

6. A jug holds 6 L of water. If there are 4 people using the jug, how many milliliters of water can each have?

_____

7. From a 2 L container of juice, 750 mL is spilled. How much juice is left?

_____

Test Prep

8. Which is the greatest capacity?

A. 2,000 mL   **B.** 2 L   **C.** 3 L   **D.** 3,200 mL

9. **Writing in Math** James says that there are 5,000 mL in 50 L. Is he correct? Explain.

_____

_____

_____

Larry's Dog When Larry was in fourth grade, his dog gained
7 lb. The dog was sick over the summer and lost 3 lb. When
Larry started fifth grade, his dog weighed 81 lb. How much did
Larry's dog weigh when Larry started fourth grade?

Read and Understand

Step 1: What do you know?

The dog weighed 81 lb when Larry started fifth
grade. The dog gained 7 lb when Larry was in
fourth grade, and lost 3 lb over the summer.

Step 2: What are you trying to find?

How much Larry's dog weighed when Larry
started fourth grade

Plan and Solve

Step 3: What strategy will you use?

Strategy: Work backward

Draw a picture to show each change.

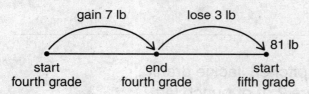

Start at the end, work backward using the
opposite operation of each change.

Where the dog gained weight, I subtract. Where
the dog lost weight, I add.

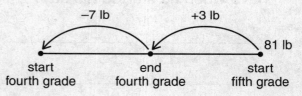

81 lb + 3 lb = 84 lb

84 lb − 7 lb = 77 lb

The dog weighed 77 lb when Larry started fourth
grade.

Look Back and Check

Step 4: Is your answer reasonable?

Yes, I worked backward using the weights that were known.

1. Cristie spent $6.50 on food and $22.50 on a haircut. She
   had $5.00 left. How much money did she have before she
   spent any?

   _____

   _____

Name_____

Work Backward

Solve each problem. Write the answer in a complete sentence.

1. This morning 50 mL was poured out of a container of water. Then 1 L of water was added, making the total amount of water 1,500 mL. How much water was in the container before any was poured?

_____

_____

2. Marty has $6.25 at the end of the day. Today he bought lunch for $8.50, a bagel for breakfast for $1.25, a newspaper for $2.25, and a necklace for his mother for $37.75. He was paid $12.50 for delivering two boxes of paper to his uncle's office. How much money did Marty have when he started his day?

_____

_____

3. Cindy drank 4 c of fruit punch from a pitcher. Jackie drank 2 c and Lauren drank 2 more. There are 2 qt of punch left in the pitcher. How many quarts of punch were there before the girls drank some?

_____

_____

4. It took Will 30 min to walk from his house to the grocery store. He was in the store for 45 min, and then walked for 15 min more to his grandmother's house. It was 3 P.M. when he arrived at his grandmother's. What time did Will leave his house?

_____

_____

Customary Units of Weight

The reference book weighs 3 lb. How many ounces is that?

3 lb = _____ oz

1 lb = 16 oz

3 × 16 oz = 48 oz

3 lb = 48 oz

So, the reference book weighs 48 oz.

23 oz = _____ lb

Think of 23 oz as 16 oz + 7 oz.

Then you can replace 16 oz with 1 lb.

23 oz = 16 oz + 7 oz

23 oz = 1 lb 7 oz

So, 23 oz = 1 lb 7 oz.

Choose the better estimate for each weight.

1. banana
8 oz or 8 lb

_____

2. car
1,000 lb or 1,000 oz

_____

3. egg
1 oz or 1 lb

_____

4. cat
10 lb or 10 oz

_____

Find each missing number.

5. 5 lb = _____ oz

6. 19 oz = _____ 1 lb _____ oz

7. 2 lb 3 oz = _____ oz

8. 37 oz = _____ lb _____ oz

9. 10 lb = _____ oz

10. 1 lb 5 oz = _____ oz

11. Number Sense Which is greater, 161 oz or 10 lb?

_____

Name_____

Customary Units of Weight

Choose the better estimate for each weight.

1.

   3 lb or 3 oz _____

2.

   30 oz or 30 lb _____

3.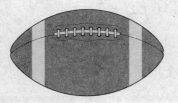

   2 lb or 2 oz _____

Find each missing number.

4. 48 oz = _____ lb

5. 4 lb = _____ oz

6. 1 lb 2 oz = _____ oz

7. 22 oz = _____ lb _____ oz

8. 3 lb 4 oz = _____ oz

9. 41 oz = _____ lb _____ oz

Test Prep

10. How many ounces are in 9 lb?

    A. 118   **B.** 128   **C.** 144   **D.** 156

11. **Writing in Math** Jane wanted to find out how many pounds there are in 42 oz. She knows there are 2 lb, but is not sure what to do next. Explain how to finish the problem.

    _____

    _____

    _____

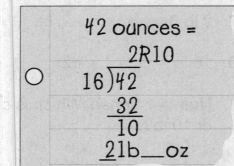

42 ounces =

2R10
16)42
32
10

2 lb __oz

Grams and Kilograms

Grams and kilograms are the metric units to tell how heavy an object is. 1 kg is equal to 1,000 g. A gram is about as heavy as a paper clip.

How to change between grams and kilograms:

To convert from kilograms to grams, you multiply by 1,000.	To convert from grams to kilograms, you divide by 1,000.
2 kg = _____ g	4,000 g = _____ kg
1 kg = 1,000 g, so 2 kg = 2 × 1,000 g	4,000 g ÷ 1,000 = 4 kg
2 kg = 2,000 g	4,000 g = 4 kg

Choose the better estimate for each.

1.  150 g or 3 kg

_____

2.  1 kg or 1 g

_____

Find each missing number.

3. 5 kg = _____ g   **4.** 8,000 g = _____ kg

5. 6 kg = _____ g   **6.** 12 kg = _____ g

7. 7,000 g = _____ kg   **8.** 9 kg = _____ g

Name_____

Grams and Kilograms

Choose the better estimate.

1.

    3 g or 3 kg _____

2.

    40 kg or 400 g _____

Find each missing number.

3. 40 kg = _____ g

4. 16,000 g = _____ kg

5. 9 kg = _____ g

6. 14 kg = _____ g

7. 4,000 g = _____ kg

8. 7,000 g = _____ kg

9. **Number Sense** Which is less, 7,500 g or 9 kg? _____

10. **Number Sense** Which is greater, 8,100 g or 10 kg? _____

11. Eight new crayons weigh a total of 1,200 g. If each crayon
is the same weight, how much does each crayon weigh? _____

Test Prep

12. How many grams are in 9 kg 20 g?

    A. 110   **B.** 920   **C.** 1,100   **D.** 9,020

13. **Writing in Math** Explain whether you would use grams or
kilograms to weigh a letter.

_____

_____

_____

_____

Temperature

On the Fahrenheit scale, water freezes at 32°F and boils at 212°F. At 32°F you would need a winter parka, gloves, and a warm hat if you were planning to go outdoors.

On the Celsius scale, water boils at 100°C and freezes at 0°C. At 32°C, you would wear shorts and a T-shirt.

How to read a thermometer

The top of the column is at 80 on the Fahrenheit scale, so the temperature is 80°F. The top of the column is at about 28 on the Celsius scale, so the temperature is about 28°C.

Write each temperature using °C.

1.

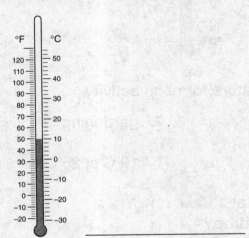

2.

_____

Write each temperature using °F.

3.

4.

_____

Name_____

Temperature

Write each temperature using °F.

1.  _____

2.  _____

Write each temperature using °C.

3.  _____

4.  _____

Estimate Choose the better outdoor temperature for each activity.

5. jogging

20°C or 40°C

6. sledding

17°F or 40°F

7. gardening

10°C or 25°C

8. If it is 84°F at noon on Monday and 70°F at 11 P.M. on Monday, how much did the temperature drop?

Test Prep

9. Which is the best temperature for snow skiing?

A. 40°C   **B.** 10°C   **C.** 40°F   **D.** 10°F

10. Writing in Math Would you describe the temperature as cold, warm, or hot if it were 35°C? Explain.

_____

_____

_____

Name_____

Describing Chance

You can use the words **certain**, **likely**, **unlikely**, or **impossible** to describe the chance that something will happen.

If you were to toss the number cube to the right:

It is **certain** that you would toss a number from 1 to 6, because all of the numbers are between 1 and 6.

It is **likely** that you would toss a number greater than 1. There are 5 numbers that are greater than 1, and there is 1 number that is not greater than 1.

It is **unlikely** that you will toss a 6. There are 5 numbers that are not 6, and one number that is 6. The event does not have a good chance of happening, but it could.

It is **impossible** that you would toss the number 7, because there are no 7s on the cube.

Describe each event as certain, likely, unlikely, or impossible.

1. There are no pencils in the school.   _____

2. Moe the cat can play the trumpet.   _____

3. Next week will have 7 days.   _____

4. Janet's dog has 4 legs.   _____

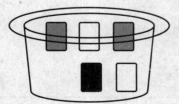

Suppose you pick a card from the hat without looking.
Describe each pick as certain, impossible, likely, or unlikely.

5. Picking a shaded card   _____

6. Picking a round card   _____

7. Picking a card that is not a black card   _____

Name_____

Describing Chances

Sarah is an adult with a dog named Fred. Describe each event
as certain, likely, unlikely, or impossible.

1. Fred will sleep tonight. _____

2. Fred will weigh more than Sarah. _____

3. Fred will eat. _____

4. Fred will learn to play the accordion. _____

Describe each spin as certain, impossible,
likely, or unlikely.

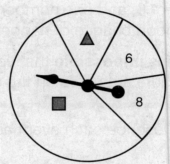

5. Spinning a square _____

6. Spinning a triangle _____

7. Spinning an even number _____

8. Spinning an odd number _____

Test Prep

9. Which is the best description of the event that a cat will
   become a doctor?

   A. Likely   **B.** Unlikely   **C.** Certain   **D.** Impossible

10. **Writing in Math** Explain the difference between a likely
    and an unlikely event.

    _____

    _____

    _____

    _____

Fair and Unfair

Spinner X

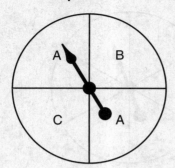

Spinner Y

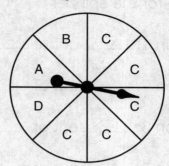

Spinner X has 4 sections.

There is a 1 out of 4 chance that Spinner X will land on the letter B.

There is a 2 out of 4 chance that Spinner X will land on the letter A.

Spinner Y has 8 sections.

There is a 1 out of 8 chance that Spinner Y will land on the letter A.

There is a 5 out of 8 chance that Spinner Y will land on the letter C.

Give the chance of each outcome.

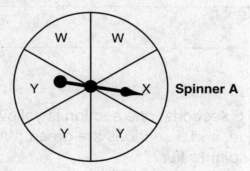

Spinner A

1. the letter W _____ out of _____

2. the letter Y _____ out of _____

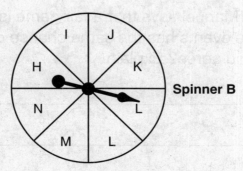

Spinner B

3. the letter H _____ out of _____

4. the letter L _____ out of _____

Name_____

Fair and Unfair

Use the spinner for 1–4. Give the chance of
each outcome for the spinner.

1. Landing on 1: _____ out of _____

2. Landing on 2: _____ out of _____

3. Landing on 3: _____ out of _____

4. Landing on 4: _____ out of _____

5. **Reasoning** In a game with two people, the players take
   turns tossing a six-sided number cube with the numbers 1, 2,
   3, 4, 5, and 6. Player 1 wins if the toss is less than 3. Player 2
   wins if the toss is 3 or more. Is the game fair? Explain.

_____

_____

_____

Test Prep

6. In a spinner with 6 sections, one section is yellow,
   2 sections are blue, and 3 sections are green. Which
   would make the spinner fair?

   A. Change a blue section to yellow   **B.** Change a green section to yellow

   C. Change a blue section to green   **D.** Change the yellow section to green

7. **Writing in Math** Manuel says that a fair game is one in
   which each of the events has the same chance of
   happening. Do you agree? Explain.

_____

_____

_____

Probability

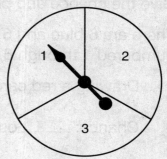

Probability can be written as a fraction. The denominator of the fraction is the number of possible outcomes and the numerator is the number of favorable outcomes.

If you want the spinner to land on a 1, then landing on a 1 is the favorable outcome. The probability of the spinner landing on a 1 is $\frac{1}{3}$.

If you want the spinner to land on a number greater than 1, then the favorable outcomes are landing on a 2 or landing on a 3.

The chance of landing on a number greater than 1 is 2 out of 3.

The probability of the spinner landing on a number greater than 1 is $\frac{2}{3}$.

A number cube has the numbers 10, 20, 30, 45, 51, and 60 on its sides.

Give the chance and probability of each event.

1. Tossing a number that is even

Chance: _____ out of _____

Probability: $\dfrac{\Box}{6}$

2. Tossing a number that ends in 0 or 1

Chance: _____ out of _____

Probability: $\dfrac{\Box}{\Box}$

3. Tossing a number less than 30

Chance: _____

Probability: $\dfrac{\Box}{\Box}$

Probability

Give the chance and probability of each event.

There are 6 blue and 6 red color cards. Each color has cards numbered 1 through 6.

1. Drawing a red card

Chance: _____ out of 12

Probability: $\dfrac{\rule{1.5cm}{0.4pt}}{12}$

2. Drawing a card with a 5

Chance: _____ out of _____

Probability: $\dfrac{\rule{1.5cm}{0.4pt}}{\rule{1.5cm}{0.4pt}}$

A 12-sided number cube has the numbers 1 through 12 on the sides. Give the probability of tossing

3. an even number. _____

4. a number greater than 9. _____

5. the number 6. _____

6. a 3, 6, 9, or 12. _____

A bag contains 6 marbles: 3 are green, 1 is yellow, and 2 are blue.

7. What is the probability of drawing a green marble? _____

8. What is the probability of drawing an orange marble? _____

Test Prep

9. What is the probability of spinning an even number?

A. 2 out of 4

B. $\frac{1}{4}$

C. $\frac{2}{4}$

D. $\frac{3}{4}$

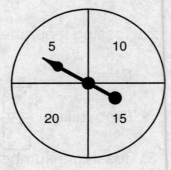

10. Writing in Math Explain the probability of one event in a fair game with three possible outcomes.

_____

_____

_____

Name_____

Writing to Explain

Which Cube? Joe and Mona each took 10 turns tossing the number cubes below. Use the results of their tosses to predict which of the two number cubes below they most likely used. Explain how you made your prediction.

Number Cube A: 2, 4, 7, 13, 16, 21   Number Cube B: 6, 12, 16, 24, 30, 31

Results of Number Cube Experiment

Name	Times even number was tossed	Times odd number was tossed
Joe	9	1
Mona	8	2

Writing a Math Explanation

- State your prediction.

- Use information from the problem to help explain your prediction.

- When a problem has choices for the answer, explain why some of the answers are not chosen.

- Use specific examples or numbers to explain why something makes sense.

Example

I think the children used *Number Cube B*.

The table tells me that most of the tosses were even numbers. *Number Cube B* has more even numbers on it than *Number Cube A*. More tosses would be even using *Number Cube B*.

1. Karl predicted that if he spun the spinner to the right 100 times, it would land on the letter X about the same number of times as it landed on the letter Z. Do you agree? Explain.

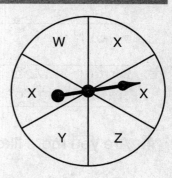

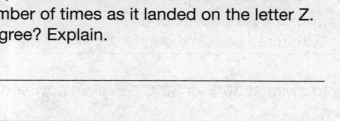

Name_____

Writing to Explain

Write to explain.

1. Explain why the spinner is not fair.

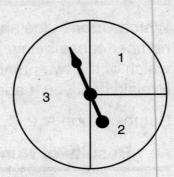

_____

_____

_____

2. A bag contains tiles with the letters shown. Explain how to find the probability of drawing a letter tile that is not a vowel.

_____

_____

_____

3. Is it likely, unlikely, certain, or impossible that the sun is shining somewhere? Explain your decision.

_____

_____

_____

4. Are you more likely to swim at 30°F or 30°C? Explain how you decided.

_____

_____

_____

PROBLEM-SOLVING APPLICATION
Mr. Tomato Juice

Donato runs a small factory that makes tomato juice. He sells the tomato juice in 5 gal containers. How many quarts are in 5 gal?

You know that there are 4 qt in a gallon, so multiply 5 by 4 to find the number of quarts.

$5 \times 4 = 20$, so 5 gal = 20 qt.

1. A local restaurant ordered 9 gal of tomato juice. How many quarts is that?

   _____

2. Donato puts a very small amount of water in each gallon of tomato juice he makes. Would he put in 3 L or 3 mL?

   _____

3. Each container of Donato's tomato juice weighs about 8 lb. How many ounces is that?

   _____

4. To make his tomato juice, Donato first boils a large amount of water. About how many degrees Fahrenheit would the water be when it is boiling?

   _____

5. Donato finished making a batch of tomato juice at 9:15 A.M. It took him 10 min to season the batch. Before that, he cooked and mixed it for 1 hr. At what time did he begin making the batch?

   _____

6. To make a special batch of tomato juice, Donato adds 3 c of vegetable juice to the mix. How many pints of vegetable juice does he add?

   _____

Name_____

Marble Probability

Suppose you pick a marble from the bag shown at the right without looking.

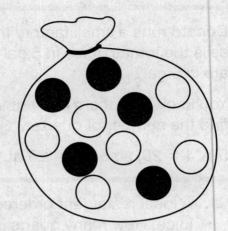

1. What is the probability that the marble you draw is a white marble?

   _____

2. What is the probability that the marble you draw is a black marble?

   _____

3. What color marble would you need to add to make the game fair? Explain how you decided.

   _____

   _____

   _____

   _____

After adding the marble to make the game fair, what is the probability of drawing

4. a white marble? _____   5. a black marble? _____

6. Suppose each marble that is in the bag shown above weighs 3 oz. How much will the marbles weigh altogether in pounds and ounces? Explain.

   _____

   _____

   _____